The People's Celebration of the Eucharist

Fintan Lyons OSB

Published by Messenger Publications, 2024

Copyright © Fintan Lyons OSB, 2024

The right of Fintan Lyons OSB to be identified as the author of the Work has been asserted by him in accordance with the Copyright and Related Rights Act, 2000. All rights reserved. No part of this book may be reproduced or utilised in any form or by any means electronic or mechanical including photography, filming, recording, video recording, photocopying or by any information storage and retrieval system or shall not by way of trade or otherwise be lent, resold or otherwise circulated in any form of binding or cover other than that in which it is published without prior permission in writing from the publisher.

Scripture quotations are taken from the New Revised Standard Version Updated Edition. Copyright © 2021 National Council of Churches of Christ in the United States of America. Used by permission. All rights reserved worldwide.

ISBN: 9781788126892

Designed by Brendan McCarthy
Typeset in AGaramondPro-Regular and Sabon LT Pro
Printed by Hussar Books

Messenger MJP Publications
www.messenger.ie

37 Leeson Place, Dublin D02 E5V0
www.messenger.ie

For Mabel and all lovers of the Mass

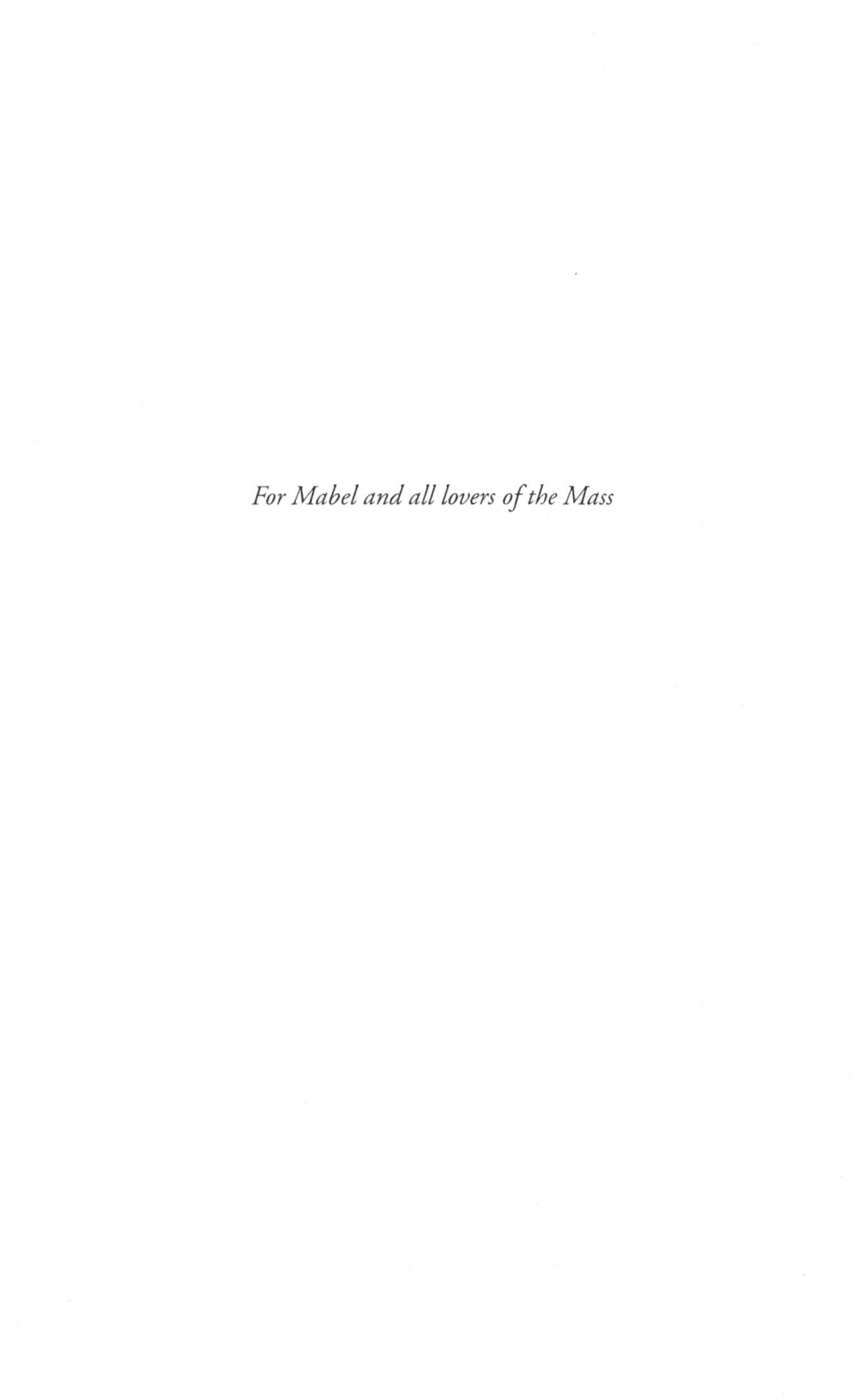

Contents

Foreword 7

Introduction 9

1: Who Are the People? 16

2: Who Were the People? 36

3: What Are the People Celebrating: a Meal,
   a Sacrifice, or both? 54

4: How Can the People Express Their Eucharistic Belief? 69

5: How Can the People Celebrate Today? 86

Epilogue 105

Acknowledgements 111

Foreword

To present an easily read and short but reasonably adequate reflection on the mass is a challenge, and I am hoping this work will succeed. I was drawn into the attempt by casual conversations with members of a group that had been described as 'non-theological', but nonetheless turned up for a talk on what was listed as 'the theology of the eucharistic celebration'. Some felt their starting point was curiosity, but also a degree of puzzlement; the liturgical changes after the Vatican Council had clouded some of the certainties of their catechism days and challenged them to find new and better ones. People were left with a desire for stability, a graspable understanding of what the mass is about

In an earlier book, *Food, Feast and Fast: From Ancient World to Environmental Crisis,* I had dealt with the Eucharist from the standpoint of people's needs in a world where climatic change threatens food production and food and other forms of production in turn are causing climate change. The focus of this book is narrower and the amount of the 'fruits of the earth' involved quite small, but people today must celebrate the Eucharist with a sense of responsibility for the welfare of the planet.

In the years before the Second Vatican Council (1962–65), there was an abundance of popular literature about the mass. But there were also more technical studies in which the Western liturgy in general was effectively described as jejune, compared with the ornate style of the Eastern Churches' liturgy, with 'jejune' having implications of questionable simplicity and brevity. Not everyone shared that view; about 1902, Hilaire Belloc, after attending mass in a crowded village church in France on the Feast of Corpus Christi, commented approvingly in his book, *The Path to Rome*: 'The mass was low and short, they are a Christian people.'[1]

In Ireland too, the mass was often low and short and appreciated for that very fact. In a country where the Catholic ethos was almost tangible and the practice rate extremely high, devout Catholics' experience of the mystery of the mass was often intense, but because of human limitations (on the part of faithful and priest) best not prolonged. It may have been a way of coping with the pressures exerted by an increasingly secular world, where compartmentalisation seemed necessary to keep one's spiritual equilibrium. An early morning mass left one right for the day.

Then came the Second Vatican Council. Compared with the way things had been, the Council represented a paradigm shift. One result of it was the declaration in the Decree on the Ministry of Bishops:

> [They should] constantly exert themselves to have the faithful know and live the Paschal Mystery more deeply through the Eucharist and thus become a firmly-knit body in the unity of the charity of Christ.[2]

This book is a modest attempt to assist in that task.

Endnotes
1. Hilaire Belloc, *The Path to Rome* (Harmondsworth: Penguin Books, 1958), p. 45.
2. *Christus Dominus* (Vatican: The Holy See, 1965), 15.

Introduction

The title of this small book, *The People's Celebration of the Eucharist*, needs an explanation. I have written it from a conviction that there is an urgent need to provide an accessible account of the great mystery at the heart of faith: Christ's saving presence among us in the eucharistic celebration. The Eucharist is more than just a rite performed by a priest in the presence of a congregation, although for many centuries it was seen by so many to be just that. Today, when Christian belief in general is at a discount, it is difficult to maintain that simple faith of the past. The challenge is to explore what being together at mass means and to find a language to express it. In other words, it is the *people's* celebration of the Eucharist that is the focus of this book, but just how inclusive is that term, 'the people', and how real is the celebration? These questions are not as straightforward as they might appear!

I start from the idea that the celebration of the Eucharist, when viewed as an activity of the People of God, the Body of Christ, allows both *ordained* and *non-ordained* to be taken as one.[1] According to the Greek Orthodox theologian, John Zizioulas, baptism and confirmation have the nature of an ordination: the baptised person takes a particular place in the *ordo*, the way the eucharistic assembly is arranged or ordered. 'Once this is forgotten, it is easy to speak of the laity as non-ordained.'[2] This Orthodox understanding is not emphasised in the Western tradition, which made little use of the word '*ordo*' until the theology of the sacraments began to emphasise the uniqueness of the priesthood. As will be seen in chapter 1, baptism is central to identifying who 'the people' of this book's title are.

A new, yet very old, language emerged from the deliberations of the Second Vatican Council (1962–65) as a solution to the issue of participation in the mass, and this language will be at the core of the book. Fundamentally, it is scriptural language, but as it derives from the New Testament letters of St Paul and others, it is not likely to be familiar to those who do not read Scripture regularly. Paul used it to describe God's plan for the salvation of all creation through Christ's life, death and resurrection. It is important to note the reference to the resurrection.

The central term in this new language, one that figures largely in the Council's Constitution on the Liturgy, *Sacrosanctum Concilium*, is the 'Paschal Mystery of Christ', an inclusive term that sums up Christ's saving of the world through his life, death and resurrection. The mass is the making present of his action; to describe the mass as a celebration of the Paschal Mystery is to refer not only to Christ's sacrifice on the cross but also to his resurrection. This perspective on the celebration is much more comprehensive than the age-old understanding of the mass as the sacrifice on Calvary made present. The mass always was a celebration of the Paschal Mystery, but that fact was obscured by the emphasis on Christ's death, as the large crucifix over the altar in many churches indicated.

It is extraordinary and hard to understand why so long after the Vatican Council catechesis in schools and parishes has not caught up with the Council's teaching, with the result that so many of the faithful have never heard the term 'Paschal Mystery' nor of its implications for understanding what is celebrated in the mass.

The Catholic Catechism has in fact has a lucid description of it:

> [The Paschal Mystery] is a real event that occurred in history, but it is unique: all other historical events happen once, and

then they pass away, swallowed up in the past. The Paschal mystery of Christ, by contrast, cannot remain only in the past, because by his death he destroyed death, and all that Christ is – all that he did and suffered for all people – participates in the divine eternity, and so transcends all times while being made present in them all. The event of the Cross and Resurrection abides and draws everything towards life.[3]

Admittedly, even that description requires close attention, but the reference to time and eternity, their interpenetration, resonates with people's instincts about the importance of the mass.

Those of us who enthusiastically set about implementing the teaching of *Sacrosanctum Concilium* almost sixty years ago were probably at fault for not realising that what we knew from *Sacrosanctum Concilium* was not known to people generally, and we focused too much on the implications of the bland English term 'active participation'. As a result, how profound the term 'participation' is, how inclusive the term 'people', and how real the term 'celebration' were only superficially grasped.

In the centuries up to the Second Vatican Council, church authorities presumed that the faithful would be present at mass, though no active role was assigned to them. It was simply understood that the mass was worship by the whole Church. Historically, the mass had come to be seen in medieval times as a representation of Christ's Passion and the congregation began to adopt a passive stance of reverent contemplation, with the result that even the age-old practice of the Offertory procession was dropped in medieval times.[4] However, the Council of Trent in the sixteenth century taught that the faithful were called to offer their sacrifices with Christ as members of the Church, and if not present, should be represented by an acolyte to make the responses included in the text of the Missal. This would make the use of the plural form in the prayers of the mass correspond to reality.[5]

The Missal dating back to Trent provided preparatory prayers for the priest, including one in which he expressed explicitly his intention to celebrate the mass. It helped him to focus his mind on the meaning of what he was about to do.[6] A large crucifix with a figure of the suffering or dead Christ usually hung over the altar as a clear illustration of the sacrificial nature of the rite, with no hint of the resurrection. Along with the cross-emblazoned chasuble and complicated ceremonies, this contributed considerably to creating a reverent silent atmosphere. Many books were published containing devotions for use by the people while the priest celebrated the mass.

Today many books are available on the role of the 'congregation', the body of faithful, who gather with the presiding cleric for the worship of God. These books focus in the main on the ways in which the faithful may contribute to the performance of the rite. They emphasise a collaborative model, using the words 'priests and people', for example, but may conceal the shortcomings of terms used. For example, the use of the word 'laity' to describe the faithful is technically inappropriate, because the Greek root of the word has a comprehensive meaning, 'all the people', including the clergy.

Even though much has changed since the Second Vatican Council, the problem of the participation of the faithful in the celebration of the Eucharist has endured. Several generations after the Council, there are many individuals and groups who think the Mass should not have been changed at all. In an article published ten years after the Council, the novelist, Evelyn Waugh, a convert to Catholicism, expressed his strong preference for the way things had been:

> Of the extraneous attractions of the Church, that which most drew me was the spectacle of the priest and his server at low mass, stumping up to the altar without a glance to discover how many or how few he had in his congregation; a craftsman and his apprentice; a man with a job which he alone was qualified to do. That is the mass I have grown to know and love.[7]

The zeal, perhaps, of a convert and the picture of a man going confidently about his task has a certain appeal, but cradle Catholics may have a different perspective on those days: loyal attendance at a ritual with half-heard Latin words that lulled the less attentive into a state of pious boredom, until bells alerted them to the high point, the elevation. It was clear well before the Second Vatican Council that, in the modern world with its many distractions, the participation of the 'non-ordained' in a celebration centred on a priest with his back to them needed to be reassessed.

Pope Francis, in his Apostolic Letter *Desiderio Desideravi*, reacted to the praise for things past and complaints about the Council's programme of liturgical renewal. In referring to 'the Paschal Mystery' he has in mind today's official understanding of the current rite of the mass, which some say lacks a 'sense of mystery'.

> When I speak of astonishment at the Paschal Mystery, I do not at all intend to refer to what at times seems to me to be meant by the vague expression 'sense of mystery'. Sometimes this is among the presumed chief accusations against the liturgical reform. It is said that the sense of mystery has been removed from the celebration. The astonishment or wonder of which I speak is not some sort of being overcome in the face of an obscure reality or a mysterious rite. It is, on the contrary, marvelling at the fact that the salvific plan of God has been revealed in the paschal deed of Jesus (cf. Eph 1:3–14), and the power of this paschal deed continues to reach us in the celebration of the 'mysteries', of the sacraments. … If the reform has eliminated that vague 'sense of mystery', then more than a cause for accusations, it is to its credit. Beauty, just like truth, always engenders wonder, and when these are referred to the mystery of God, they lead to adoration.[8]

This book is about the changes introduced by the Council but also about their limitations, especially when the role of the people is considered in depth. Establishing just who 'the people' are and what it means when we talk of the 'celebration' of the Eucharist will help us to make sense of both the changes wrought by the Council and the challenges of implementing them.

The plan of this book
The first chapter is about how comprehensive the concept of 'the people' actually is, when the Eucharist is celebrated. It will explain the term 'Paschal Mystery', the key concept for the understanding of the eucharistic liturgy.

The second chapter will consider the 'breaking of the bread' in the early Church's practice and the way in which it developed up to St Augustine in the fifth century, including his critique of the use and abuses of his day. In effect, this will introduce consideration of the historical process that gave a relatively fixed shape to the celebration and eventually caused the meal dimension to diminish in significance over the centuries.

The third chapter will deal with the *nature of the celebration*, namely, the question of *what* the people were and are celebrating, thereby introducing the debate about sacrifice and meal as interpretations of the Eucharist. I will discuss the characteristics of a meal as a human event. This chapter will range over centuries and practices.

The fourth chapter will deal with the question of what Christ's presence in the celebration means, including controversial theological opinions. I will assess relevant official church documents. The chapter will also draw on insights gained from Orthodox liturgical practice.

The fifth and final chapter will return to the issue of participation in light of the current situation of widespread use of digital platforms to access the celebration. I will introduce the issue of the presence of the end-time, as an aspect of the celebration not much in evidence today. The chapter will deal also with pastoral issues related to the traditional understanding of Sunday and present-day culture, including attitudes to the 'weekend' and the working week. In light of the situation where the Church can be seen as a little flock more than a great people, I will return to the custom known as the *agape* meal of the early Christian centuries, briefly mentioned in chapter two, and discuss its relevance to pastoral practice today.

Endnotes

1. See, Yves Congar, 'The Structure of Christian Priesthood', in *At the Heart of Christian Worship: Liturgical Essays of Yves Congar,* trans. and ed by Paul Philibert (Collegeville: Liturgical Press, 2010), p. 74.
2. John D. Zizioulas, *Being as Communion* (Crestwood, NY: St Vladimir's Seminary Press, 1993), pp. 215–6: '(It) must be stated emphatically that there is no such thing as a "non-ordained" person in the Church. Baptism and especially confirmation, as an inseparable aspect of the mystery of Christian initiation involve a "laying on of hands". ... The East has kept these two aspects not only inseparably linked with one another, but also with what follows, namely the Eucharist. The theological significance of this is that it reveals the nature of baptism and confirmation as being essentially an ordination, while it helps us understand better what ordination itself means. As we can see already in Hippolytus' *Apostolic Tradition,* the immediate and inevitable result of baptism and confirmation was that the newly baptised would take their particular place in the eucharistic assembly ... (become) a member of a particular *ordo* in the eucharistic assembly. Once this is forgotten, it is easy to speak of the laity as "non-ordained".'
3. *Catechism of the Catholic Church*, 1085.
4. For the late medieval period, see Gregory Dix, *The Shape of the Liturgy* (London: A. & C. Black, 1945), p. 599: 'The part of the individual layman in that corporate action, had long been reduced from *doing* to *seeing*. ... Now it is retreating within himself to *thinking* and *feeling*.'
5. Exceptions were made over the centuries allowing a priest to celebrate without an acolyte. This was to facilitate monks who lived as solitaries.
6. The prayer was composed and added to the Missal by Pope Gregory XIII (1572–1585).
7. Evelyn Waugh, letter to the editor, *Catholic Herald*, 7 August 1964.
8. Pope Francis, *Desiderio Desideravi* (Vatican: The Holy See, 2022), 25.

1: Who Are the People?

This chapter addresses the surprising question of just who 'the people' are who celebrate the mass. The Second Vatican Council's call for the renewal of the Church's worship implied that changes were needed from the practice going back many centuries, when descriptive language could be that the priest *offered*, or *said*, or *read* mass and the ordinary people *attended*, or *got* mass, or satisfied their obligation. In the official terminology of the time, the English word 'celebrate/celebration' was used in relation to performing the rite, not necessarily to imply solemnity but a term reflecting the Latin term *celebrare* used in the Missal and related contexts. The Latin term's basic meaning is derived from *celeber*, meaning 'crowded' and has no religious connotation, but *celebrare*/celebrate was used in relation to the mass, because the rite was meant to be one with a body of people attending. (The English word, 'celebrity', has the same background – someone who draws a crowd.) In today's world, there is quite a lot of emphasis on celebration on the part of those who have the means to afford it; it is not surprising that people who hold belief in the Eucharist should aspire to celebrate it well.

The faithful who 'congregate' today for the celebration are *considered as united* with the presider in the act of performing the ceremonies of the rite contained in the Roman Missal, which was issued in 1970 to implement the decisions of the Vatican Council. It also marked, not quite by chance, the 400th anniversary of the Missal produced in 1570 to implement those of the then recent Council of Trent. The word 'mass' is the most familiar way of naming that celebration, and the name is derived from a Latin word, *missa*, which was one of the final words said by the priest when the mass was in Latin, '*Ite, missa est*' – in English: 'Go, the mass is ended.' Strange, it might seem, that this small word came to designate the whole service, but it had been from early times a technical term to indicate the completion of some other liturgical ceremonies.

The Missal of today was the first fruits of the Vatican Council's programme of renewal. It is prefaced by a 'General Instruction', not often read by priests or the faithful; it uses part of paragraph no. 57 of *Sacrosanctum Concilium*, the Constitution on the Liturgy, to express the nature of the eucharistic celebration:

> At the Last Supper our Saviour instituted the Eucharistic Sacrifice of his Body and Blood, by which he would perpetuate the Sacrifice of the Cross throughout the centuries until he should come again, thus entrusting to the Church, his beloved Bride, the memorial of his death and resurrection.

It is somewhat unfortunate that the complete paragraph from the constitution is not included in the 'General Instruction', as it goes beyond the concept of sacrifice to include that of banquet or meal. The text concludes with

> a sacrament of love, a sign of unity, a bond of charity, a paschal banquet in which Christ is eaten, the mind is filled with grace, and a pledge of future glory is given to us.

It is true that the word 'banquet' is used several times in the 'General Instruction', but using it rather than the word 'meal' tends to put the reception of the Eucharist in a category that obscures the reality that physical eating and drinking is what actually occurs. To include the people in a fully human sense in a rite involving bread and wine, the aspect of a meal is required.

Sacrosanctum Concilium

Changes in the way of celebrating the mass were mandated by *Sacrosanctum Concilium*, which was introduced by the Second Vatican Council as part of its general programme of renewal of the life of the Church. This involved recognising that some practices, rituals and attitudes apparently hallowed by tradition should be questioned and altered, and brought up to date in the sense of assessing them in light of modern needs and sensibilities. It involved also looking back to the early centuries of the Christian era, to draw on the wisdom and understanding of the Church's way of life.

Sacrosanctum Concilium was the first document of the Council to be agreed upon, at the first session of the Council in 1962. It was influenced by developments both pastoral and doctrinal in the first half of the twentieth century. Pope Pius X had advocated more frequent reception of the Eucharist in 1903, and Pope Pius XII had issued the encyclicals *Mystici Corporis* (1943) and *Mediator Dei* (1947). In both encyclicals, the term 'mystery' was prominent, though *Mediator Dei* dealt at length with the saving mystery of Christ's death celebrated in the liturgy, his sacrifice, without mentioning his resurrection. It included condemnation of those who had the 'temerity and daring ... to make use of the vernacular in the celebration of the august eucharistic sacrifice'.[1]

The Preparatory Commission on the Liturgy, which gathered before the Council, introduced the more general term 'the mystery of the sacred liturgy' in its deliberations in 1960. This paved the way for the introduction of the term 'Paschal Mystery', to describe Christ's passion, death and resurrection, in *Sacrosanctum Concilium*.[2]

Development of the understanding of the nature of the Church

For the full implications of the ideas and recommendations of *Sacrosanctum Concilium* to be understood, development of the Council's teaching on the nature of the Church was needed. In 1963, *Lumen Gentium*, the Constitution on the Church, was published. In *Lumen Gentium* the mysterious nature of the Church was emphasised over against the standard view up to that point, which understood the Church as an institution in society, a visible, perfect one lacking nothing required for its completeness[3] and with a divinely appointed authority structure consisting of pope, bishops and priests, guiding and regulating the life of the faithful.

The teaching of the Church after the sixteenth-century Council of Trent gradually adopted the position that membership of the Church required the external profession of orthodox faith, attendance at the Church's worship and acceptance of the authority of the hierarchy, a markedly external test and a position strongly orientated towards seeing the Church as a visible body. In the unfortunate simile used by the early seventeenth-century Cardinal Bellarmine, the Church was 'as visible as the Republic of Venice'.

When the Council formulated its teaching in *Lumen Gentium*, the first chapter was devoted to the Church's spiritual nature and the third to its institutional structure, the image that had been dominant.[4] After much debate, a statement about the Church, taking account of both chapters, was agreed by all but a few bishops:

> (The Church of Christ) constituted and organised in the world as a society, subsists in the Catholic Church, which is governed by the successor of Peter and by the bishops in communion with him, although many elements of sanctification and of truth are found outside of its visible structure. These elements, as gifts belonging to the Church of Christ, are forces impelling toward catholic unity.[5]

This description already has implications for who can be said to belong to the community of the Church at worship. Acknowledging that elements belonging to the reality of the Church existed outside the boundary of the Catholic Church was a decisive step away from the traditional position, which did not accord any recognition to the

Churches and Christian communities resulting from the sixteenth-century Reformation: the Anglicans, Methodists, Presbyterians, for example. The debate and reasoning that led to the use of the word 'subsists' was summarised by an ecumenical expert, Cardinal Willebrands, in a subsequent lecture about the council debate:

> A short phrase proposed by the German bishops and the Scandinavian episcopal conference gives the crux of the whole argument: 'No one can be Christ's without belonging to the Church.' But the body of Christ is the Church. The conclusion is that whoever belongs to Christ belongs to the Church, and hence that the limits of the Church are coextensive with those of belonging to Christ.[6]

This emphasis on the Church as the Body of Christ has implications for the extent to which others might be numbered among the people when the celebration of the Eucharist is being considered. This situation was considered further in the second chapter of *Lumen Gentium*, 'On the People of God'. That chapter introduced a new perspective on the nature of the Church and established a bridge between the Church as mystery of chapter one and the institutional Church of chapter three in the form of an image rooted in the Old Testament's teaching on the covenant between God and his chosen people, Israel. It presented the image of the Church as a pilgrim people, with an emphasis on God's saving action down through history, and thus an image of a Church moving towards its destiny, when the kingdom of God is fully established, an image of incompleteness but also of presence because of Christ's victory over death, his resurrection.

In the new covenant established by Christ, the People of God became 'a kingdom of priests to his God' (Apoc 1:6).[7] This priestly status comes about through baptism, as the quotation from John Zizioulas in the introduction asserted. It has implications for how extensive this people is, given that baptism is the mode of entry to all Christian communities, whether in communion with the Catholic Church or not. The chapter acknowledges that

> this messianic people, although it does not, in fact, include everybody, and at times may seem to be a little flock, is a most certain seed of unity, hope and salvation for everybody.[8]

It also acknowledges that

> to it (the People of God) belong or are related in different ways, the catholic faithful, others who believe in Christ and finally all of humankind called by God's grace to salvation.[9]

Further on it says,

> the Church has many reasons for knowing that it is joined to the baptised who are honoured by the name of Christian, but do not profess the faith in its entirety or have not preserved unity of communion under the successor of Peter.[10]

How extensive is the concept 'the people'?
Taken together with the Council's teaching on the 'subsistence' of the Church in the Catholic Church and its relations with other Christians, the People of God model raises the issue of how extensive this people is. Given that the baptised non-Catholic Christian communities celebrate the Eucharist in various forms, the question arises as to what their status as people of God implies in relation to the Catholic Eucharist. Cardinal Willebrands expressed his conviction in that regard:

> The baptism that (an ecclesial) community celebrates is a baptism which incorporates in Christ within that community. There are no vagrant baptised … It is in the community, Lutheran, Methodist or Baptist, etc., that grace is given, and belonging to the Church takes place there.'[11]

The logic of his position is that in those communities the celebration of the Eucharist, as well as baptism, can confer grace, depending on what the community expressly believes in relation to the Eucharist.

However, to what extent they may participate in the celebration of the Catholic Church's Eucharist is another issue. It is a contentious one now, because in fact at Catholic celebrations hospitality is on occasion extended to other Christians, even with official permission when certain conditions are observed. In today's situation of shrinking numbers of practising Catholics and often a great sense of *esprit de corps* among those still loyal, attitudes vary as to whether strict regulations should apply or a more permissive policy be adopted. There is anecdotal evidence that in places worldwide where repressive regimes persecute Christians, believers are more inclined to share their faith and their worship.

Sacrosanctum Concilium set out ways in which the faithful fulfilled their role. The 'divine sacrifice of the Eucharist', the constitution declared, 'is supremely effective in enabling the faithful to express in their lives and portray to others the mystery of Christ and the true nature of the church'.[12] Of itself, this did not imply anything more than the reverent silent participation that had characterised the mass in the centuries after the Council of Trent. It did not enlarge at that point on 'the mystery of Christ', and introduced the word 'Eucharist' without noting that it is the Greek word for giving thanks, though together these terms will be the key to developing a deeper view of what it means to talk about the people's celebration of the Eucharist.

Active participation

> Mother Church earnestly desires that all the faithful should be led to that fully conscious and active participation in liturgical celebrations, which is demanded by the very nature of the liturgy. Such participation by the Christian people as 'a chosen race, a royal priesthood, a holy nation, a redeemed people' (1 Pet 2:9; cf. 2:4–5) is their right and duty by reason of their baptism.[13]

There has been debate since the Second Vatican Council about what 'active participation' implies, how physically active it should be and not simply passive though attentive. Long before the Council, Pope

Pius X had used the exact term (in Italian) in his *motu proprio*, *Tra le Sollecitudini* (1903) on the liturgy, though for him it seems to have no more comprehensive a meaning than that the faithful should unite themselves spiritually with the liturgical rite performed by the priest-presider.[14] There is a helpful reference in *Sacrosanctum Concilium* to the faithful's 'active participation, internal and external in the liturgy, taking into account their age, condition, way of life and standard of religious culture'.[15] Recognising internal participation implies that it need not always mean a physical action such as bringing up gifts in a procession, but the implementation of the constitution's directive has in practice resulted in various active roles being filled by the faithful in the celebration of the Eucharist and of the sacraments.

People have long been aware that 'active participation' is now asked of them, and naturally think of this in terms of performing the readings, bringing up the gifts, acting as what is officially described as Extraordinary Minister of the Eucharist. But people may not actually have understood in depth what 'participation' actually is. It is more than fulfilling roles or listening to the readings and adverting to the meaning of the prayers, though these are part of participation. The Prayer of the Faithful, restored after the Second Vatican Council, was of great importance as an expression of the people's participation in the early Church's liturgy and can be given greater prominence today by having it prepared in advance by members of a liturgical group in the parish.[16]

To know what really is being asked of the people requires an understanding of the Paschal Mystery. People need to know that this is what is celebrated in the Eucharist and then endeavour to participate in its celebration.

The Paschal Mystery

To enlarge on *Sacrosanctum Concilium*'s reference to the 'divine sacrifice of the Eucharist' and 'the mystery of Christ'[17] requires extending the term 'mystery of Christ' by adding 'Paschal'. The term 'Paschal mystery of Christ' is in fact found quite often in it and in other Council documents. It is derived from the terminology used by Paul in his letters to describe God's plan for the salvation of all creation through Christ's life, death and resurrection. The term 'Paschal Mystery' is central for understanding the Eucharist today and, fortunately, the Catholic Catechism has a particularly lucid description of it.

> [The Paschal Mystery] is a real event that occurred in history, but it is unique: all other historical events happen once, and then they pass away, swallowed up in the past. The Paschal mystery of Christ, by contrast, cannot remain only in the past, because by his death he destroyed death, and all that Christ is – all that he did and suffered for all people – participates in the divine eternity, and so transcends all times while being made present in them all. The event of the Cross and Resurrection abides and draws everything towards life.[18]

In his Apostolic Letter, *Desiderio Desideravi*, Pope Francis referred frequently to the Paschal Mystery, saying, for example, that it was not enough for us to have a vague memory of the Last Supper; we have need to be present at it, and this is brought about by the celebrating the liturgy of the Eucharist:

> In the Eucharist and in all the sacraments we are guaranteed the possibility of encountering the Lord Jesus and of having the power of his Paschal Mystery reach us.[19]

The Paschal Mystery, the whole reality of Christ's life, death and resurrection, is made present and effective as a source of saving grace, when the People of God celebrate the Eucharist. Pope Francis underlined the reality of the experience by his comment:

> If there were lacking our astonishment at the fact that the Paschal Mystery is rendered present in the concreteness of sacramental signs, we would truly risk being impermeable to the ocean of grace that floods every celebration.[20]

It becomes present in time when priest and people in a community, representing the whole Church, come together to celebrate the Eucharist. The Penitential Rite prepares the community 'to celebrate the Sacred Mysteries' and the Opening Prayer which follows marks the beginning at a particular moment in time of a celebration of the eternal Paschal Mystery.

The greeting by the presider should reflect the reality of the fundamental oneness of priest and people, so it is not appropriate for him to welcome the faithful who are present; it is after all their own house, recognised as such in the Gaelic tradition by the term *teach an phobail*. (There are of course special circumstances, such as the visit of a group not normally present; a welcoming word can make it clear that they too belong.)[21] We need to remember that it is God the Father, through Christ, and in the unity of the Spirit, who welcomes us to a foretaste of the banquet of the kingdom described in Isaiah 25:6:

> On this mountain, the Lord of hosts will provide for all peoples feast of rich food and choice wines, juicy, rich food and pure, choice wines.

The 'now and not yet' nature of the celebration, its relation to God's final reign, is important, and I will consider that aspect of it in the final chapter. But from the beginning, an act of worship that participates in Christ's Paschal Mystery is taking place.

According to *Sacrosanctum Concilium*, there are various perspectives from which Christ himself is believed to be present. He is present in the proclaiming of the Word, in the priest as his representative and 'lastly, when the Church prays and sings, for he has promised: "Wherever two or three are gathered together in my name, there am I in the midst of them" (Mt 18:20)'.[22] The use of the word 'lastly' does not seem appropriate when introducing the Church's prayer and singing, which is actually the Church's celebration of the Paschal Mystery. In fact, a deeper understanding of the Church as celebrant needs to take account of the relationship between Christ and the

Church, his body, and thereby come to the realisation that Christ himself is the celebrant, as the theologian Yves Congar explained:

> There is a profound unity between the physical body of the Lord, crucified and risen, his sacramental body offered in the Eucharist and his ecclesial body which offers itself up. ... It follows that the whole Church, as People of God and Body of Christ, celebrates the spiritual worship, both personal and communal, inaugurated by Jesus Christ, of which he remains the chief celebrant.[23]

Christ is present in multiple aspects before the point in the mass comes where the bread and wine become his body and blood, because from the beginning Christ's Paschal Mystery is being celebrated.

Eucharist
The word 'Eucharist' is appropriate for the celebration as the rite is an act of thanksgiving for Christ's saving activity. The word helps to distinguish the current rite from that in the Missal published in 1570, where the emphasis was on the mass as a *sacrifice* offered by the priest, with little attention to thanksgiving or to the role of the people. The rite was in Latin and had its origin in decisions of the sixteenth-century Council of Trent. The word 'Eucharist' in today's Missal designates the central part of the rite, the eucharistic prayer, which exists in a variety of versions. As thanksgiving, the term can quite reasonably be extended to designate the entire celebration, including the Liturgy of the Word and the Rite of Communion. To talk of the celebration of the Eucharist is to highlight this central prayer, recited by the priest alone, but it is reasonable to speak of the people's eucharistic celebration. Within the eucharistic prayer, the word 'we' often occurs.

The action, however, of the members of the Body of Christ in union with its Head implies that at a profound level ordained and 'non-ordained' are on a basically equal footing, though in the discussions at the Council a perception affecting the relation between the faithful and the presider had come to the fore. In *Lumen Gentium*, the Council declared:

> Though they differ from one another in essence and not only in degree, the common priesthood of the faithful and the ministerial or hierarchical priesthood are nonetheless interrelated: each of them in its own special way is a participation in the one priesthood of Christ.

In a study of equality in the Christian life, and critical of that paragraph, Thomas O'Loughlin stated:

> Within the Trinitarian dynamic of Christian life, the notion of equality has sound foundations. The Father's love is impartial and is with us in our creation, we become children of the Father in baptism and 'we put on Christ' whether we be male or female, Jew or Greek, slave or free.[24]

The role of the priest

In addition to the distinction introduced in *Lumen Gentium* between the 'common priesthood of the faithful' and the 'ministerial or hierarchical priesthood',[25] the term *in persona Christi* (in the person of Christ) was associated especially with the priest presider in *Sacrosanctum Concilium*. Originally *in persona* was used in classical Latin to describe a legal process by which a person could act on another's behalf. It acquired theological import from the early Christian centuries onwards, with the meaning that a person spoke in and through another. By medieval times the term *in persona Christi* was ascribed to the priest presider. Christ was speaking or acting through him. This usage appears twice in *Sacrosanctum Concilium*:

> [T]he prayers addressed to God by the priest who presides over the assembly in the person of Christ are said in the name of the entire holy people and of all present.[26]

This quotation acknowledges the fact that the entire Body of Christ (the holy people) addresses the Father, and it is therefore accurate to say that the entire holy people acts *in persona Christi*. However, in the *Decree on the Ministry and Life of Priests*, the Council in one of its final documents introduced a new term, *in persona Christi capitis* (Christ the Head), to identify the priest presider and retain the distinction between him and the people. However, taking all the references to 'priest and people' and their relationships into account in the Council's documents, it seems reasonable to conclude that 'the people's celebration of the Eucharist' should not be understood only as the contribution of the faithful to the celebration but is a more comprehensive term including also the presider.

It has to be said that Pope John Paul II in his teaching added emphasis to the conception of the priest as acting *in persona Christi*; he declared that the phrase *in persona Christi*

> means more than offering 'in the name of' or 'in the place of' Christ. *In persona* means specific sacramental identification with the eternal High Priest.[27]

His concern was to emphasise that the identity of the priest was more than being empowered to act as the representative of the people; he could not be seen as acting simply in *persona ecclesiae.*

He made this view clear with the statement:

> The ministry of priests who have received the sacrament of Holy Orders, in the economy of salvation chosen by Christ, makes clear that the Eucharist which they celebrate is *a gift which radically transcends the power of the assembly* and is in any event essential for validly linking the eucharistic consecration to the sacrifice of the Cross and to the Last Supper.[28]

According to a study published in *Studia Canonica*, the background to this insistence by Pope John Paul II on the identity of the priest probably comes from a perceived need to safeguard the traditional teaching confining the priesthood to men.[29]

Challenges of translation
The programme of renewal of the liturgy following the Council took place early in Pope St John Paul II's pontificate and proceeded with his approval. Some reservations in its regard were current in his time and became influential during the pontificate of Benedict XVI. Without deliberate intent on the part of those responsible for the revised texts following the Council, some texts did in fact favour a less comprehensive understanding of the term 'people'. For example, in the 1970 Latin Missal, many of the core texts from 1570 inevitably remained unchanged and reflected an understanding that left the role of the priest dominant in many places, but *Sacrosanctum Concilium* also mandated the translation of the Missal into vernacular languages. The translation into English was undertaken by a commission that had to decide how to express the Latin of the text in English in a way reflective of contemporary language in the countries that would use the Missal. The technique employed was called 'dynamic equivalent' and accordingly not always a literal translation.

The use of English presented a new opportunity to many to participate more 'consciously' in the celebration, including a new awareness that it was a celebration, but it also caused issues to arise, which those opposed to the changes could point out to justify their position. At the beginning of the rite, the English text was not a literal translation but 'And also with you', where the literal translation would be 'And with your spirit'. While the translation used had a simplicity about it, it did not reflect the traditional emphasis on the 'Spirit filled' role of the priest. There were other simplifications, which the majority of the faithful might not notice, but opponents of change would.

From 1998 on into the new millennium, opposition to the translation in this and in other respects built up at influential levels, including the Vatican Congregation for Divine Worship, the body responsible for the liturgy. Following a ruling it issued in the document *Liturgiam Authentican* in 2001,[30] the English translation was replaced in the years 2010 and 2011 by one adhering strictly to literal translation from the Latin of the Missal. In at least two significant places, the new translation distinguished more obviously between the roles of the priest and the people. Where the previous translation had used 'our sacrifice' in the Offertory text, it now, as a literal translation from the Latin, became 'my sacrifice and yours'. The English translation of Eucharistic Prayer I, also called the Roman Canon, used at one point the words 'we your people and your ministers' and this was corrected to 'we your servants and your holy people', a literal translation of the Latin. The English translators' wish to emphasise the communal nature of the celebration had led to the inversion of the order and the omission of the word 'holy', presumably because the phrase runs more smoothly without it.

A more subtle aspect of the literal translation in use now affects the sense of the mass being a people's celebration. It uses hieratic or priestly language, an elevated style resulting from the sober, dignified nature of the Latin language, which were formulated in the early Christian centuries.[31] It is difficult for people to listen to and make sense of the syntax and the classical allusions of the literally translated text. This leaves the priest to struggle with complex sentences, when he is endeavouring to express the sentiments of the people. There were many complaints from liturgical scholars about this change to a literal translation, because of the verbal infelicities and the awkwardness of syntax.[32]

Online participation
In an account by Justin Martyr in the second century, discussed in detail in chapter two, the group celebrating the Eucharist consisted of people who were Christians gathered in from 'town or country', but the fact that the Eucharist was brought to others not present means that these also belonged and celebrated even though in a retrospective way. The practice continues today, as officially deputed people bring the host to those confined to their homes. The term 'people' is not then restricted to those physically present, and this gives rise to an issue today.

To what extent then are online participants in the celebration members of 'the people' who are celebrating the Eucharist? Two basic principles need to be taken into account. First a local celebration can be described as a celebration of the 'domestic Church' to distinguish and identify it within the universal Church, the 'one holy, catholic and apostolic Church', which is really the worshipping body at all times, according to Vatican II. The whole Church celebrates the Eucharist, and this has implications for online participation. The other principle is that as a sacrament the Eucharist consists of two elements, words and material elements. It is something tactile and finds its completion in the act of eating and drinking. That act can be completed (usually only through eating) by people not physically present, when deputed ministers bring the Eucharist to them. In that way, they can be considered members of 'the people' who celebrate.

Those watching the action via a webcam or other medium are obviously in a different situation, yet if they are Christians, who at the visible level accept the traditional criteria for membership of the Church, they can be regarded as participating in some sense in the celebration, despite the reservations mentioned above in relation to online participation. In this case, a practice from former times, when people were physically present but did not receive the elements, is worth noting, as people in that situation were usually said to make a 'spiritual communion'. In a period embracing the twelfth and thirteenth centuries, there were convents of enclosed nuns who lived at such an ascetic and mystical level that many experienced a sensation in the mouth and a sense of union with Christ without actually receiving the host physically. A thirteenth-century Cistercian nun, Ida of Louvain, had this experience according to her biographer:

> It frequently happened that when the priest received the holy communion at the altar ... she in the intensity of her desire received with her mouth at the selfsame moment the most sacred pledge of the host of the Saviour (brought we believe by a ministering angel) and discerned with the sense of taste and even chewed with her teeth.[33]

There are devout people today who, while physically present or via a webcam, rely on the idea of 'spiritual communion', though not in such an extraordinary way as that of Ida of Louvain. This is an important point, because witnessing remotely a live well-presented celebration could give the impression that this is as fully a grace-filled activity as being physically present and receiving communion.

Secularism

Physical presence at the celebration of the Eucharist does not necessarily guarantee participation. For example, consider those present who do not believe in the Eucharist in the way the Church requires, or at all, or those present who have debarred themselves by a life that cuts them off from the Body of Christ. In Chapter 15 of John's Gospel, Jesus described himself as the vine, and his disciples as branches drawing life from him. He also warned: 'Whoever does not abide in me is thrown away like a branch and withers' (Jn 15:6).

The influence of secularism in today's culture can give rise to a lack of sensitivity to one's spiritual status and to indifference to the ethos of a church celebration, allowing someone to be present and see it as little more than a social gathering to celebrate an event, such as a wedding. This is more likely to occur today compared with times past, when a sense of the sacred attached to church buildings themselves, and there was a felt need for quietness on the part of those present in church for a wedding for funeral.

Yet the need to reach out to people who, for whatever reason, are separated from the worshiping community has been stressed by Pope Francis in his role as the chief pastor seeking out the sheep that are lost. When people gather for the celebration of the Eucharist on special occasions, such as a wedding or a funeral, there is need for great sensitivity on the part of the presider and the members of the community who are true believers, but know there are others present who do not share that status. Such a grace-filled occasion may create a sense of need to be part of the celebration in people who know they are alienated but feel a desire to share with their believing companions; they may find that such an occasion is moving them gradually towards belief. Similarly, research in some non-Catholic communities has found that many feel a desire to belong rather than to be 'saved', the core concept in evangelicalism.

There are religious communities who make a much clearer distinction between those who belong and those who do not, whether it is in relation to attendance at services or the choice of marriage partners, and this is true also of some branches of Orthodox Christianity. There are also communities of Evangelical Christians who welcome 'others' to take part in services, but make it clear that doing so does not mean that such outsiders can regard themselves as actually belonging. This situation is described as 'fencing the table', meaning that admission to communion is not open to outsiders. These are generally minority groups in relation to the Christian community in general.

In the years before the Vatican Council, when the Catholic Church more obviously identified itself as a visible society with hierarchical structure and well-marked boundaries of belonging, the issue of who could be part of the people's celebration of the Eucharist was more easily determined. Outward profession of the faith sufficed for participation in the Church's services on the part of people not excluded by excommunication, even though a person's actual status in relation to faith and Christian living could not be verified. The situation is more complicated today because of the greater number of nominal Catholics, those who identify in surveys as Catholic, but do not attend services. It remains to be seen what strategy the Catholic community will adopt if in the future it increasingly self-identifies as a minority in society.

Conclusion
The question as to who may be considered part of the people who celebrate the Eucharist is more complicated today because of the number of nominal Catholics, those who identify in surveys as Catholic but do not have the faith necessary to participate, even if on occasion they attend services. There is the issue too of the extent to which participation can take place online – I will return to this

very important issue in the last chapter. The extent to which other Christians may really participate in the liturgy, if their faith is in accordance with Catholic teaching, is also important; official policy may on occasion allow it, and the extent to which it actually occurs cannot be known. Taking the view that the community of practising Catholics can be for practical purposes considered 'the people', I want now to consider their participation by looking back to the early centuries, when it was easier to know who the people were.

Endnotes

1. Pope Pius XII, *Mediator Dei* (Vatican: The Holy See, 1947), 59.
2. Joseph Komonchak, 'The Liturgical Commission', in *The History of Vatican II*, vol. 1, ed by Giuseppe Alberigo, J. Komonchak (Maryknoll, NY: Orbis, 1995), p. 206.
3. See Avery Dulles SJ, *Models of the Church: A Critical Assessment of the Church in All its Aspects* (Dublin: Gill and Macmillan, 1976), p. 31.
4. That understanding was the basis of what was planned by officials in Rome as a comprehensive document on the Church, prepared in advance of the Council, but not, as it turned out, accepted by the gathering of bishops from around the world.
5. *Lumen Gentium* (Vatican: The Holy See, 1964), 8.
6. Jan Cardinal Willebrands, 'Address to the National Workshop for Christian Unity', Atlanta, Georgia, 5 May 1987, in Pontifical Council for Promoting Christian Unity, *Information Service*, N. 101 (1999/II–III), 146.
7. *Lumen Gentium*, 10.
8. *Lumen Gentium*, 9.
9. *Lumen Gentium*, 13.
10. *Lumen Gentium*, 15.
11. Willebrands, 'Address to the National Workshop', pp. 148–9.
12. *Sacrosanctum Concilium* (Vatican: The Holy See, 1963), 2.
13. *Sacrosanctum Concilium*, 14.
14. Jozef Lamberts, 'Pope Pius X and Active Participation', *Worship*, 97 (October 2023), 300–323.
15. *Sacrosanctum Concilium*, 19.
16. See Paul de Clerck, '*The Universal Prayer*' *in the Latin Liturgies: Patristic Evidence and Liturgical Texts*, trans. by Jennifer O'Brien (Turnhout: Brepols, 2024).
17. *Sacrosanctum Concilium*, 2.
18. *Catechism of the Catholic Church*, 1085.
19. Pope Francis, *Desiderio Desideravi*, 11.
20. Pope Francis, *Desiderio Desideravi*, 24. See Neil Xavier O'Donoghue, 'Redeemably Awful: The Paschal Mystery', *The Furrow*, 71:6 (2020), p. 343: 'If the Paschal Mystery of the Death and Resurrection of Christ is not *front* and *central* to the liturgical experience in a parish, it is impossible to find Christ's promised fulness of life in the liturgy.'

21. In many US parishes, a member of the ministry team welcomes those who are there for the first time and invites them to register as parishioners, if that is appropriate.
22. *Sacrosanctum Concilium*, 7.
23. Yves Congar, *At the Heart of Christian Worship*, trans. and ed by Paul Philibert (Collegeville, MN: Liturgical Press, 2010) p. 18.
24. Thomas O'Loughlin, 'Equality as a Theological Principle within Roman Catholic Ecclesiology', *Ecclesiology*, 18 (2022), p. 51, and p. 52: 'The liturgy of baptism brings it clearly home to the new disciple that the Church is a community of equality – wealth and status should bring no special favour here. But, of course, we love gathering privilege around us and this is what happened at the Eucharistic meals at Corinth. ... There have been endless "corrections" of liturgical practice down to our own time.'
25. *Lumen Gentium*, 10.
26. *Sacrosanctum Concilium*, 33; the other use is at *Sacrosanctum Concilium*, 7.
27. Pope John Paul II, *Ecclesia de Eucharistia*, 28
28. Pope John Paul II, *Ecclesia de Eucharistia*, 29, emphasis in text. 'The assembly gathered together for the celebration of the Eucharist, if it is to be a truly Eucharistic assembly, absolutely requires the presence of an ordained priest as its president.'
29. Serena Noceti, '*In persona Christi*: Limits and Potential of an *espressione abusata*', *Studia Canonica*, 56 (2022), 441–470, reconstructs 'the underlying interpretative framework and the intentionality' expressed in the magisterial documents of Pope John Paul II concerning *in persona Christi* and sees in them an attempt to justify confining priestly ordination to men. See especially pp. 447–9.
30. *Liturgiam Authenticam*, 20 decreed: 'the original (Latin) text, insofar as possible, must be translated integrally and in the most exact manner, without omissions or additions in terms of their content, and without paraphrases or glosses.'
31. Ansgar Chupungco, 'History of the Roman Liturgy until the Fifteenth Century' in *Handbook for Liturgical Studies*, vol. I, ed by Ansgar Chupungco (Collegeville: Liturgical Press, 1997), p. 138.
32. There were many complaints from liturgical scholars about this change to a literal translation, but they centred on the verbal infelicities, on awkwardness of syntax resulting from adherence to literal translation. In 2016, Pope Francis responded to this situation by setting up an enquiry, which is ongoing.
33. Caroline Bynum, *Holy Feast and Holy Fast: The Religious Significance of Food to Medieval Women* (Berkeley: University of California Press, 1987), p. 117.

2: Who Were the People?

Looking back to the early centuries of the Church for an appropriate way to describe the celebration of the Eucharist, we find that the early Christians got on with the 'breaking of the bread', the usual name for the rite, without concern for leaving an explanatory record of what they were doing for the benefit of later generations. After the coming of the Holy Spirit at Pentecost, they were initially a tightly knit community, according to the Acts of the Apostles:

> They devoted themselves to the apostles' teaching and fellowship, to the breaking of bread and the prayers. Day by day, as they spent much time together in the temple, they broke bread at home and ate their food with glad and generous hearts, praising God and having the goodwill of all the people. (2:42, 46–7)

Those verses follow immediately after one that records the baptism of about three thousand, resulting from Peter's preaching, so it is seems that the practice of breaking bread in their homes became an extensive occurrence, as well as did gathering in the temple area, where area indicates the temple environs. Evidently, in this new way of life, they looked back to the Last Supper when Christ had said, 'This is the new covenant in my blood. Do this in memory of me', as he spoke of his coming death, according to Luke's Gospel and Paul's First Letter to the Corinthians. The fundamental elements that go to make up our celebration today were there from the beginning: a sacrifice offered in the course of a meal.

The Last Supper
The three synoptic gospels, Matthew, Mark and Luke, refer to Jesus instructing his disciples to prepare for the Passover meal, a rite laid down in Exodus 12:1–4 and used in Jewish tradition to commemorate and bless God for the liberation of Israel from slavery in Egypt. John's Gospel (18:28; 19:14, 31) implies, however, that the Last Supper took place in the period before Passover and the Crucifixion on the preparation day for the Passover. One scholar holds that the question is not crucial:

> (E)ven if the Last Supper *were* a Passover meal, no practices that were exclusive to that festive meal seem to have been retained in the primitive Church's eucharistic celebrations, but only those that were common to all formal Jewish meals, and even if it *were not* a Passover meal, it still took place within a Passover atmosphere and context.[1]

John's account is the more credible in that it has Jesus condemned to death at noon on the eve of Passover, at the hour when the priests were sacrificing the Paschal lambs for the evening meal that began the feast.[2] The synoptic presentation, however, was intended to establish a close connection between the covenantal rite described in Exodus and Jesus' reference to the new covenant he was introducing, and I will follow the familiar synoptic gospels' account. At the same time, the Eucharist of the early Church consisted of a simple rite involving bread and wine, with no allusion to ceremonies peculiar to the Passover festive meal.

The major feasts were example of first fruits offerings, and in this feast a lamb was a first fruit of the flock. The rite of slaughtering a lamb and a special meal at Passover were a way of marking, of celebrating, with thanksgiving the covenant between God and his chosen people, whom he rescued from slavery. There are several references to covenants between God and the Hebrew people in the Old Testament, and the disciples knew what a covenant meant, a reassuring agreement of benevolence and of course mutual obligation.

The New Covenant
The synoptic gospels say that Jesus gave his disciples instructions to prepare for the paschal celebration in accordance with custom. In their minds, it would have been a rite of thanksgiving to God for that historic event of liberation and of the covenant between God and Israel, and they did not know until he told them (Mk 14:25) that this was the last time he would take part in the rite, in effect it would be the end of the rite. He then unexpectedly introduced a new *meaning* to the standard proceedings. He blessed a loaf of bread gave it to them to be shared and said, 'This my body', and did the same with the cup, and said that his action established a *new* and eternal covenant in his blood – covenants being marked by the shedding of blood. The shedding of his blood, which was to occur the next day, replaced the covenant they had actually gathered to celebrate.

The Jewish rite required the sacrifice of a lamb; he was the new lamb of sacrifice. Sacrifice is at the heart of what Christ was initiating. As John 3:16, says 'God loved the world so much that he gave his only son', and Jesus' life on earth was one of cooperation between father and son to live the reality of that divine love by a life of goodness and truth, in the world. His life involved constant witness to truth and of combat against evil. Evil appeared to have conquered, but he rose from the dead. As an acclamation in the mass says, 'Dying you destroyed our death, rising you restored our life.' During the last phase of his life, Christ had said that he had overcome the world (Jn 16:33) and when lifted up would draw all people to himself (Jn 12:32). So we celebrate Christ's victory over evil when we celebrate the Paschal Mystery, but we know that our own victory has yet to come, even though we know too that 'just as Christ was raised from the dead by the glory of the Father, we too might walk in newness of life' (Rom 6:4).

People wonder sometimes about the timing involved in the events of the Last Supper. Jesus says, 'This my blood', though he has not yet been put to death. It can be seen as an example of proleptic language, the bringing forward verbally of an event that has not yet occurred. Preferably, it can be seen as beyond that actual historical setting, the Jewish festival of that fateful year, and instead an event belonging to God's *eternal*, timeless act of liberating humankind by the intervention of the eternal son in history – in other words, the inauguration of the Paschal Mystery. From the eternal perspective, the order of events is not a problem. The first Christians who gathered in their small communities after the resurrection knew that when they broke bread together, Christ and his saving action were present, and that what they now did had the new meaning of celebrating the new covenant between God and humankind sealed in Christ's blood.

The breaking of the bread

The breaking of the bread, without mention of the wine, was a common way of describing the eucharistic celebration in the New Testament writings. It may reflect the natural order of things, eating and then drinking. The long-standing issue of the faithful not receiving from the cup came back into discussion in the course of the reforms after the Second Vatican Council. It had already been a major issue in the century leading up to the sixteenth-century Protestant Reformation. At that time, when only the priest received both elements, and the faithful rarely received at all, this emphasised the idea of sacrifice accomplished by the priest by means of his sacred power, with the people spectators, and obviously it took away from the idea of the Eucharist being a community meal. In the Vatican II reforms, restoring the cup – in principle – for the faithful was meant to restore the idea of the celebration as a continuation of ancient practice, that of a shared meal.

To go back to the earliest days, there has been interesting speculation about lack of reference to the cup in some New Testament texts, especially regarding the evangelist Luke's reference or non-reference to it. The standard text of Luke's Gospel gives an account of the Last Supper (22:14–21) that includes the words, 'This cup is the new covenant in my blood', but some old versions of the text[3] omit the reference to the cup. It is certainly omitted in the text by Luke recording Paul and Luke's final meeting with the community at Troas in Acts 20:7–12: 'on the first day of the week, when we met to break bread'. The cup is also omitted in the account in Luke's Gospel of the meal the two disciples had with the risen Christ at Emmaus (Lk 24:25), when they recognised him in the 'breaking of the bread'. The point at issue is why Luke may have avoided mentioning this part of what would become the normative performance of the rite of the Eucharist. Diverse views among researchers who have examined other aspects of the life of the early Christian community, especially of the strongly ascetical groups, have resulted in no agreed opinion among scholars as to why Luke seems to avoid mentioning wine.[4]

While in later centuries the Eucharist is clearly a rite involving bread and wine, the situation is not so simple with regard to the practice of the early Church. Ascetics who would not approve of wine drinking, as well as unorthodox groups who subscribed to esoteric ideas about diet and beliefs, might well have looked for different ways of celebrating the memory of Christ, including the use of bread and water. The Ebionites were a group of this kind, an early Jewish-Christian sect.[5] St Cyprian of Carthage, who was martyred in 258, seems to have been referring to them when he wrote 'against the custom of certain persons' to his brother, Caecilius, about the necessity of wine and water for the Eucharist. The wine represents Christ's blood, the water the people:

> Thus the cup of the Lord is not indeed water alone, nor wine alone, unless each be mingled with the other.[6]

He developed a cogent argument involving wine, water and even bread and flour:

> When we consecrate the cup of the Lord, we cannot offer water alone, any more than we can offer wine alone. If we offer wine alone, the blood of Christ is present but without us; if the water is alone, then the people are there alone, without Christ. But when the one is mingled with the other, and the two fuse to become one, then the spiritual heavenly mystery is accomplished. The cup of the Lord, then, cannot contain water alone or wine alone, but only a mixture of the two, just as the body of the Lord cannot be flour alone, but only a mixture of the two that is required for making bread.

When referring to bread, Cyprian had in mind Paul's saying, 'Because there is one bread, we who are many are one body, for we all partake of the one bread (1 Cor 10:17) as he continued:

> Here we find the unity of the Christian people represented: Just as many grains are brought together, ground and mixed so as to form a single loaf, so in Christ the heavenly bread, there is, as we well know, only one body, and with it our multiplicity is united and fused.[7]

These texts from the third century are relevant to the celebration of the Eucharist today, even though it might seem that the issue of water and wine does not arise, nor the bringing together of many grains to form bread. A small amount of water is added to the wine at the Offertory, and regulations have always required that the amount be quite small lest the wine be so diluted as no longer to be described as wine. The words said *sotto voce* by the presider are, however, very important:

> By the mystery of this water and wine, may we come to share in the divinity of Christ, who humbled himself to share in our humanity.

It is a prayer evoking the Paschal Mystery by which we become one with Christ.

Cyprian's insistence on the mixture of water and wine was to ensure that the people be united with Christ in the offering of his sacrifice, 'the sacrifice of the Lord is not properly celebrated, unless our gift and sacrifice correspond to the passion'.[8] The people must participate in the celebration of the Paschal Mystery – to use present day language. This would be clearer today if the presider drew attention to that simple rite by saying the words at a normal volume and with some degree of ceremony. Admittedly, the words quoted above, which are an ancient formula, do not fully express our sharing in the Paschal Mystery but do draw attention to the role of the people.

There is also the issue of the bread and Cyprian's reference to the single loaf. It will be seen that in papal Rome in the fourth and succeeding centuries, the bread of the Eucharist was brought in loaves for the celebration, so it was not a case of a single loaf. In early medieval Ireland a large plate, such as the Derrynaflan Paten, held a large loaf, which at a certain point in the celebration would be divided according to markings inscribed on the paten. In present day celebrations, people rarely witness the unity of the bread and its subsequent division, the breaking of the bread, despite the importance of the rite as symbol of the Eucharist's unifying function for the members of the community.[9]

There was also a clearly heretical group, the Artotyrites in Galatia in the second century, who used cheese (perhaps yoghurt) alongside bread at the Eucharist. Their name comes from the Greek words for bread and cheese. Augustine (and Thomas Aquinas) referred to them, explaining that their reasoning was that the first humans offered sacrifice using the products of the earth and of the flock. There is evidence from the period of the Carolingian Empire (ninth century onwards) that warnings were issued by authorities against the use of other than the basic elements of bread and wine, but, according to one contemporary writer, 'for many early medieval Christians, it is apparent, Eucharists of bread with water, honey, milk or another drink were perfectly valid'.[10]

The Eucharist in the context of a meal

In Paul's First Letter to the Corinthians, there is an account of a meeting of the Church there to celebrate and consolidate their community life with a meal, which concluded with a celebration of the Eucharist. This shows a further development of the Christian community compared with the gathering described in the Acts of the Apostles quoted at the beginning of this chapter, where a meal and 'the breaking of the bread' are presented as a unity.

> Now in the following instructions I do not commend you, because when you come together it is not for the better but for the worse. For to begin with, when you come together as a Church, I hear that there are divisions among you, and to some extent I believe it ... When you come together, it is not really to eat the Lord's supper. For when the time comes to eat, each of you goes ahead with your own supper, and one goes hungry and another becomes drunk. What! Do you not have homes to eat and drink in? Or do you show contempt for the Church of God and humiliate those who have nothing? (1 Cor 11:17–18; 20–22)

He was critical of the behaviour of factions within the Corinthian community who went ahead with eating their own food, instead of being a united community, when they came together to strengthen their communal bond and to celebrate what he called the 'Lord's Supper'. A possible reason for such division is that in the Christian community there were slaves as well as free people, and the slaves would be likely to have prepared the meal that the free people enjoyed, before they could enjoy their own.

The significance of this is that the Eucharist was a special ritual meal and could be distinguished from the earlier part of the proceedings, a meal celebrated in accordance with the culture of the time. In fact, in chapter 13 of this letter, Paul devotes much attention to love (*agape*) as of the greatest importance in building up the community, and it is known that the practice grew of having meetings for this purpose that were distinct from the celebrations of the Eucharist, or a meal could be held in conjunction with the Eucharist, as may be the case of the event described in chapter eleven of the Letter to the Corinthians.

Sometimes described as 'one of the most sublime passages in the Bible',[11] chapter 13 of Paul's First Letter to the Corinthians was inserted by him between the already completed chapters 12 and 14, as Paul thought it necessary to distinguish charity clearly from other gifts of the Christian life he had already described. It was not the same as philanthropic love or humanitarian concern for others (v. 3). The word he used for it, *agape*, meant disinterested, self-sacrificing love. He gave a detailed description of it:

> Love is patient; love is kind; love is not envious or boastful or arrogant or rude. It does not insist on its own way; it is not irritable; it keeps no record of wrongs; it does not rejoice in wrongdoing but rejoices in the truth. It bears all things, believes all things, hopes all things, endures all things. Love never ends. (1 Cor 13:4–8)

That love never ends distinguishes it from the passing spiritual gifts such as speaking in tongues (1 Cor 13:1). 'And now, faith, hope and love abide, and the greatest of these is love' (1 Cor 13:3).

His exhortation, inspired ultimately by God's eternal love revealed in the life of Jesus, aimed at guiding the community's way of life, as it was in fact one prone to division. Not much earlier, the life of the original Jerusalem community was described in the Acts of the Apostles as one of great harmony, sharing everything and eating their food 'with glad and generous hearts' (Acts 2:46). The idea of a love feast comes from that original setting and became established practice among Christian communities for several centuries.

It is important to realise too that the gathering of Christians to share a meal was part of the tradition of the Greco-Roman pagan world and of the Jewish religious world. In other words, their shared meal had a foundation in social customs and was not only derived from the bread and wine example of the Last Supper.

The Eucharist of Justin Martyr

As the number of communities increased, there is evidence that they came together in a larger group on occasion, thus creating the need for a larger assembly area than could be accommodated in one house. It is significant that Justin Martyr, in the mid-second century, says in his *First Apology* that 'an assembly is held in one place of all who live in town or country', indicating a larger than domestic setting. The motivation for such a coming together goes beyond being an *agape* event. Clearly, there is more involved than the 'love feast' bonding of the small community; the proceedings described by Justin take on the form of a Eucharist as we now know it. After readings from the records of the apostles and the writings of the prophets, the 'president' of the assembly prays over the gifts of food the members of the assembly have brought.

> Bread and a cup of water and a cup of mixed wine are brought to him who presides over the brethren, and he takes them and sends up praise and glory to the Father of all in the name of the Son and the Holy Spirit, and gives thanks at some length that we have been deemed worthy of these things from him. When he has finished the prayers and the thanksgiving, all the people give their assent by saying 'Amen'.[12]

The reference to the cup of water indicates that the celebration of the Eucharist Justin described followed a baptismal ceremony. There is no mention of table or altar, but some structure, presumably wooden, in the centre of the gathering would be required on which to place the gifts over which the 'president' made the prayer of thanksgiving.

The food to be blessed is central to the account. Though they were quoted earlier in Justin's account, there is no evidence that for the thanksgiving the presider used the words of Christ from the Last Supper.[13] Nor is it clear what was meant by the 'president', or how the presider was chosen, but logically it could be the one who presided over the community which the others came to join on Sunday. The martyr St Ignatius of Antioch used the term 'bishop' at the beginning of the second century, and Justin spoke of 'deacons', so it seems permanent roles of service to the community had emerged among what was the people's eucharistic celebration, their liturgy of thanksgiving:

> And when the president has given thanks and all the people have assented, those whom we call deacons give to each of those present a portion of the bread and wine and water over which thanks have been given and take them to those who are not present.[14]

Justin's description of the rite includes a negative statement and a contrasting one, evidently wishing to emphasise the positive, that the food becomes the flesh and blood of Christ:

> Not as common bread and common drink do we receive these; but in like manner as Jesus Christ our Savior, having been made flesh by the Word of God, had both flesh and blood for our salvation, so likewise have we been taught that the food which is blessed by the prayer of His word, and from which our blood and flesh by transmutation are nourished, is the flesh and blood of that Jesus who was made flesh.[15]

The text is not clear as to whether the transmutation (or transformation) refers to our flesh and blood or if it refers to the elements, which are changed into the flesh and blood of Jesus, but in effect it is both, as the result is union with Christ in the Paschal Mystery of his incarnation, passion and resurrection. The flesh and blood of Christ refer to the risen Christ with whom the Christian is united. In medieval times, there were theologians who held that the words said over the bread and those said separately over the cup expressed the separation of Christ's flesh and blood, in other words his death, and so completed Christ's sacrifice, as those theologians did not have the Paschal Mystery understanding, which reaches its completion in the resurrection. What the believer's communion with Christ could mean in that case was a problem, but these thinkers took refuge in the idea of Christ's divinity enabling the union with him. This would perforce be a spiritual union only involving the soul and was part of the trend away from the Eucharist having any corporal effect and different from Justin's understanding.

Justin pointed out that the gift of the Eucharist was made possible by the incarnation, the Son of God becoming flesh and blood. Just as the Word became flesh (Jn 1:14), so by the same Word the elements became his flesh and blood and the nourishment of the Christian. Otherwise the Christian being made of flesh and blood could not be assimilated into him. A generation later, St Irenaeus (died c. 202), in his argument against the Gnostics (who held a dualistic view, which made the body evil), asserted that it was the nature shared by humanity and the Word that made possible the nourishment for eternal life of the human body by consuming Christ's body and blood. The visible elements were ingested as food, food that fortified and built up the substance of human flesh, flesh capable of receiving God's gift of eternal life.[16]

There is a very important point to note here; for Justin and for Irenaeus, the reception of the Eucharist nourished the flesh and blood of the recipient. The effect was not simply confined to the spiritual life of the person. In later centuries, receiving communion, to use today's terminology, came to be seen as having only an effect on the soul, on the spiritual life of the person. It is interesting that the only clear case – I can find, at least – where the text of today's eucharistic rite acknowledges the twofold nature of the nourishment received in the sacrament occurs in the Prayer over the Gifts of the Eleventh Sunday in Ordinary Time:

> O God, who in the offerings presented here provide for the twofold needs of human nature, nourishing us with food and renewing us with your Sacrament, grant, we pray, that the sustenance they provide may not fail us in body or in spirit. Through Christ our Lord.

Cyril of Jerusalem, in the fourth century, instructing the newly baptised, wished to assure them that the effect of receiving Christ's flesh and blood went *beyond* physical nourishment. In doing so, he introduced a new way of thinking in that the material aspect, the eating and drinking, would begin to be lessened in favour of an interior or spiritual understanding.

> Having been fully assured that the seeming bread is not bread, though sensible to taste, but the Body of Christ; and that the seeming wine is not wine, though the taste will have it so, but the Blood of Christ ... strengthen your heart, by partaking of that spiritual bread and make the face of your soul to shine.[17]

Clearly, there is a perspective here that is far removed from the approach of the bread and water groups and that of the Artotyrites mentioned earlier, where the material element was central, even if frugal.

The Christian banquet

Cyril's view going beyond physical nourishment was really no more than a hint of things to come, the reality and importance of eating and drinking is still clearly witnessed to in a practice introduced by Pope Felix I, pope from 269 to 274. During a period of respite from persecution, he introduced the celebration of the Eucharist on the tombs of the martyrs, those Christians who had suffered during an earlier persecution by Emperor Valerian. Though Christianity was officially proscribed, the rite was not a small secretive one involving only the basic elements of bread and wine. It followed, though not closely, the pattern of the Greco-Roman banquets celebrated by their pagan contemporaries at the tombs of their ancestors. The Greco-Roman banquet was formal in both structure and procedure, beginning with a set form of invitation. Those invited took their places according to rules of social rank; it was a spectacle viewed by the lower classes who were not invited to partake. In the original Greek form, serious discussions took place, but in Rome, a lighter, even frivolous atmosphere sometimes prevailed.[18] The location at a tomb, even an ostentatious one, imposed some restrictions. The Christian eucharistic celebration differed from the Roman in that it was a community celebration, but was like the Greek in having readings and addresses.

By this time, the *agape* tradition for the enhancement of mutual love and the eucharistic rite had begun to separate, and so the meeting of Christians for the Eucharist could adopt some at least of the characteristics of the Greco-Roman banquet as the way of expressing their solidarity. Christian theology looked back to the Last Supper model, but the already existing banquet model in society, and some at least of its strict social norms, influenced the celebration of the Eucharist. That is one reason why it came to be presided over by a bishop, and the time was right for fixed formulas to emerge, the creation of the 'Eucharistic Prayer', the *anaphora*, as Greek was still widely used.[19] By the time of Felix, fixed forms of prayer were in use for the Eucharist. In Rome, a liturgical text that originated in the early third century, and now called *The Apostolic Tradition*, consisted of prayers not unlike those of present-day eucharistic prayers used in the mass. Jesus' own words from the Last Supper were in the text and would soon become standard in the West.

The question of leadership
Though the period of improvised prayers of thanksgiving was coming to an end, the bishop in *The Apostolic Tradition* text could vary

the text or interpolate some of his own prayers. What was changing also was the relationship between the community and those presiding, as the texts available included the rite for the ordaining of presbyters and deacons as well as the bishop, thus creating a hierarchical structure differing from what was evident in the community in Justin's time, not long previously. Inevitably once the Christians had moved from house churches to larger assemblies, a presiding figure was needed, probably the leader of the community the others joined on Sunday. He was not, it seems, given the title 'bishop' in Justin's circles.

Even in Paul's New Testament letters there had been reference to leadership in the community, for example in the case of the First Letter to Timothy (5:17), but the impression remained of the community in the various Churches being the deciding authority. Early in the second century, the bishop and martyr, Ignatius of Antioch, 'expressed the view that there could not be a Church without bishops, presbyters and deacons who are earthly icons of God the Father, the apostles and Jesus Christ in the heavenly church'.[20] In such cases, 'the people' emerged as a class apart, over against the ordained officials, elected by the assembly, though the exact nature of the relationship is not always clear.

The issue of dress was an important factor in the evolving situation. Clement of Alexandria (died c. 215) wrote that those celebrating the liturgy should wear clean and bright clothes, while Origen (died c. 253), also of Alexandria, held that the bishop should have one set of clothes for the liturgy and another when he moved among the people.[21] In the Roman world, the bishop and other ministers dressed in the clothes of the time, a white tunic, but of a better quality than those of the people. When Emperor Constantine gave Christianity official recognition in the early fourth century, he gave bishops the same status as civil magistrates, and they then dressed accordingly. Their presiding at the liturgy acquired a new appearance and, it might be said, a new authority. All of this widened the gap in the relation between the ordinary worshippers and their leaders and in how this relationship was perceived.

Augustine on abuses

Yet the custom of celebrating the Eucharist in the form of a shared meal persisted and in the next few generations some negative connotations of the term 'celebration' emerged. We know that the custom was widespread in North Africa at the end of the fourth century, because Augustine (354–430), not yet a bishop, wrote to the Archbishop of Carthage, Aurelius, in 392, complaining about the excesses involved:

> Rioting and drunkenness are so tolerated and allowed by public opinion, that even in services designed to honour the memory of the blessed martyrs – not only on the annual festivals, but every day – they (drunkenness etc.) are openly practised.[22]

Augustine was concerned that Christians were turning the celebration of the memory of the martyrs – a celebration of the Eucharist, the context makes clear – into a bacchanalian carnival. Here at the end of the fourth century, we have a different context from that of the gathering described by Justin in the middle of the second century: the practice of the shared meal is more evident, with accompanying abuses. As the celebration was over or at the tombs of martyrs, the term altar began to be relevant. The martyrs' sacrifices were being commemorated and sacrifice naturally brings up the idea of altar; it appears quite early in connection with the Eucharist. The famous martyr, Ignatius of Antioch, appealing for unity about 107, said:

> Be careful to use one Eucharist, for there is one flesh of our Lord Jesus Christ and one cup of union with his blood, one altar, one bishop.[23]

The Greek Fathers in the first four centuries sometimes used the word 'table' and sometimes 'altar' for the structure on which the Eucharist was celebrated. Augustine used the term altar in connection with a wooden structure, when describing an attack by schismatic Christians, Donatists, on the Catholic bishop, Maximianus:

They rushed upon him with fearful violence and cruel fury as he was standing at the altar, beat him savagely with cudgels and weapons of every kind, and at last with the very boards of the broken altar.[24]

Conclusion

The celebration of the Eucharist today differs very much from the practice of the early Church, and yet it has its origin in the Last Supper. I have tried to show that in the early centuries there was a gradual evolution toward the form of the Eucharist familiar today. I have described that evolution as far as the era of Augustine, the fifth century. That evolution continued beyond Augustine, however, and I will return to it in chapter four. So far descriptions of the Eucharist have referred to celebrations involving bread and wine. In the next chapter, I will look at the Eucharist's origin in the Last Supper and the emergence of the terms 'sacrifice' and 'altar' in the context of the relationship between sacrifice and meal.

Endnotes

1. Paul Bradshaw, *Early Christian Worship* (London: SPCK, 1996), p. 38.
2. Dating the Last Supper has been described as the most disputed calendric issue in the Gospels. See Raymond Brown, *The Gospel According to John XIII–XXI* (London: Geoffrey Chapman, 1971), p. 556: 'We suggest that, for unknown reasons, on Thursday evening, on the 14th Nisan by the official calendar, *the day before Passover*, Jesus ate with his disciples a meal that had Passover characteristics.' Italics are mine.
3. For example, the Codex Bezae and some of the Old Latin and Syriac versions. See Stephen Shaver, 'A Eucharistic Origins Story', *Worship*, 92 (2018), 298–317.
4. One recent view expresses what the writer described as a 'seems likely' position: 'Taken as a whole, it seems likely that Luke knows a bread-only or bread-and-water eucharistic practice and that his rejection of the culture of (blood) sacrifice that dominated the Greco-Roman world of his time leads him to avoid applying "blood" language to Christian meals.' Shaver, 'A Eucharistic Origins Story', p. 307. Another contemporary scholar disputes this view, see Andrew McGowan, *Ascetic Eucharists: Food and Drink in Early Christian Ritual Meals* (Oxford: Clarendon Press, 1999) p. 234.
5. McGowan, *Ascetic Eucharists*, pp. 144–5.
6. Cyprian, 'Letter 63.13', in *The Fathers of the Church*, vol. 51, trans. by Rose Bernard Donna (Washington: Catholic University Press, 1964), p. 211.

7. Cyprian, 'Letter 63.13', *The Fathers of the Church*, p. 202.
8. Cyprian, 'Letter 63.13', *The Fathers of the Church*.
9. In his classic work, *The Shape of the Liturgy* (London: A&C Black, 1945), pp. 78–82, Gregory Dix made the fraction a fundamental part of the four-fold description of the Eucharist.
10. Celia Chazelle, 'Mass and the Eucharist in the Christianising of Early Medieval Europe', in *Envisioning Christ on the Cross: Ireland and the Early Medieval West*, ed by Jennifer Mullins, Jennifer Ní Ghrádaigh & Richard Hawtree (Dublin: Four Courts Press, 2013), pp. 166–7.
11. See Richard Kugelman, 'The First Letter to the Corinthians', in *The Jerome Biblical Commentary*, vol. II (London: Geoffrey Chapman, 1969), p. 271.
12. Justin, *First Apology*, text in R. C. D. Jasper and G. J. Cuming, eds, *Prayers of the Eucharist: Early and Reformed* (New York: Oxford University Press, 1980), 67.3, p. 19.
13. Justin, 'First Apology', in *Ante-Nicene Fathers*, vol. 1 (Grand Rapids MI: Eerdmans, 1988), 66.1; 'The apostles, in the memoirs composed by them, which are called Gospels, have declared that Jesus gave them this injunction, that having taken bread and given thanks, He said, "Do this in remembrance of Me, this is My body;" and that, in like manner, having taken the cup and given thanks, He said, "This is My blood;" and that He distributed the bread and wine to them alone'.
14. Justin, 'First Apology', *Ante-Nicene Fathers*, 65.1.
15. Justin, 'First Apology', *Ante-Nicene Fathers*, 66.1.
16. Irenaeus, *Libri quinque adversus Haereses*, vol. II, ed by W.W. Harvey (Cantabrigiae: Typis academicis, 1857), pp. 204–5. It is worth noting that some English translations do not include that section of vol. II.
17. Cyril of Jerusalem, 'Catechetical Lectures 22', *Nicene and Post-Nicene Fathers*, vol. 7, ed by Philip Schaff and Henry Wace (Buffalo, NY: Christian Literature Publishing Co., 1894), Cf. Ps 103/4.
18. A fourth-century Roman historian, Ammianus Marcellinus, described the banquets of some Roman nobles as disorderly and resounding with entertainments. See Bertrand Lançon, *Rome in Late Antiquity*, trans. by Antonia Nevill (Edinburgh: Edinburgh University Press, 2000), p. 104.
19. Alan Bouley, *From Freedom to Formula: The Evolution of the Eucharistic Prayer from Oral Improvisation to Fixed Texts* (Washington DC: Catholic University of America Press, 1979), p. 156.
20. Frank C. Senn, *Christian Liturgy: Catholic and Evangelical* (Minneapolis: Fortress Press, 1989), p. 106.
21. Origen, *Homélies sur Levitique* (Paris: Le Cerf, 1981), 4.6, p. 182.
22. Augustine, 'Letter 22.1.3', *Nicene and Post-Nicene Fathers, First Series*, vol. 1, trans. by J. G. Cunningham, ed by Philip Schaff (Buffalo, NY: Christian Literature Publishing Co., 1887).
23. *A Dictionary of Liturgy and Worship*, ed by J. G. Davies (London: SCM, 1972), p. 4.
24. Augustine, *Letters* (Washington DC: Catholic University of America Press, 1952), 185.

3: What Are the People Celebrating: a Meal, a Sacrifice, or both?

Liturgical scholars in this postmodern era have speculated about the experience of people who gather to celebrate the liturgy. Ritual studies have shown that participants in rituals, including religious rituals, can have diverse experiences, and this is true also of the eucharistic celebration.[1] As a ritual act, it consists of offering gifts of bread and wine to God, thereby making them sacred (from the Latin *sacrum facere*), in other words, a sacrifice. Sacrifice has been part of culture throughout human history, from diverse motivations, ranging from a felt need to placate an angry deity to a desire to ensure plentiful harvests. In the Catholic celebration, some may participate in the hope of gaining grace for themselves or salvation for the departed, others may see the Eucharist simply as Christ's sacrifice and share in it by making an offering of themselves.

Whether consciously or not, what they are celebrating is the Paschal Mystery of Christ. The fact that the Paschal Mystery celebrates Christ's resurrection as well as his sacrificial death leaves the way open to considering the mass as a celebratory meal of thanksgiving for his victory over death. However, until the Second Vatican

Council, people were generally unaware that the mass was a celebration of the Paschal Mystery, as the term was hardly known. The term 'mysteries of Christ' had appeared early in the twentieth century, in the influential writings of Bl. Columba Marmion OSB in his book *Christ in his Mysteries*, based on Paul's references to the mysteries of Christ, especially in the Letter to the Ephesians. The book had a section entitled, 'The mysteries of Christ are our mysteries', making the point that the connection between the Christian and Christ established by baptism is strengthened by meditation on Christ's saving work and especially by participation in the celebration of the Church's liturgy. Meditation of that kind was not a new idea but participation in Christ's mystery in the liturgy was for many a novel one. Throughout the book, Marmion referred to the Paschal grace given to people through the mysteries of Christ, the spiritual gifts received through celebrating the Paschal Mystery, but did not use the term itself.

The spirituality Marmion was promoting influenced those who came to know his works, but a more widespread appreciation of the faithful's involvement in the mysteries of Christ only came with the documents of the Second Vatican Council. As was true of Councils of the Church throughout history, the process, termed 'reception', of the Vatican Council's teaching becoming part of the popular understanding of the Catholic culture may take generations. This is proving to be true in relation to the Council's teaching on the Eucharist; reservations and resistance to change have been and are today expressed even at the highest level about what is involved in the renewal of the liturgy.

Pope John Paul II, in an encyclical, spoke of how the liturgical reform inaugurated by the Vatican Council had greatly contributed to 'a more conscious, active and fruitful participation in the Holy Sacrifice of the altar on the part of the faithful', but he also expressed concern about some interpretations of the eucharistic rite. 'At times one encounters an extremely reductive understanding of the eucharistic mystery. Stripped of its sacrificial meaning, it is celebrated as if it were simply a fraternal banquet.'[2]

Many conservative faithful did see interest in the importance of the early tradition of the 'breaking of the bread' as failure to give full recognition to the doctrine of the mass as a sacrifice. This must indicate that those critics had never understood it in any way except that of the 'old' catechism's presentation of the mass as Calvary made present in an unbloody manner. They had not understood, not known or not accepted that after the Council the renewal of the Church's liturgy took the form not only of revising the texts used in the Eucharist and the other sacraments but also of renewed discussion of the doctrine of the Eucharist. This became, it is true, a far-reaching search for new ways of expressing the faith of the Church regarding this supreme mystery.

One of the insights resulting from the Council's discussions was the appropriateness of receiving Holy Communion under both kinds. This practice, to which no one could object except on grounds of reverential fear, could be regarded as a way of participating fully in the completion of Christ's sacrifice, but it also was a way of recognising the Eucharist as food and drink for the inner life of the Christian.

A shared meal?

Food does not have to be shared. For many centuries, the reception of the Eucharist was understood in terms of the life of the individual. As we have already seen, however, in the early Church the celebration of the Eucharist involved a shared meal, because the Body of Christ, the Church, needed to be nourished as a whole. The Christian practice built on the culture of the time, and while it had a meaning transcending the culture of that time, it nonetheless reflected the values of a truly human encounter and was a human as well as a spiritual feast. A shared meal, whether in a family or among friends, brings into prominence the bonds there are between those who participate. The word 'companion' potentially indicates a bond and mutual support, and its Latin source – bread together – indicates the role of a meal in expressing, augmenting or even creating this bond. Sharing a meal implies relationship and is generally indicative of a positive development in people's lives, even a reconciliation. It can be assumed that each Christian participant is open to others and brings to the assembly the warmth and the strengths of their personalities, thus enhancing the others' dignity and sense of self-worth. As Robert Disch remarked:

> Food is not merely something you put in your mouth and digest. Food is an occasion for a social act. It's an occasion for meeting. It's an occasion for conversation.[3]

In the original Christian communities, belief in the resurrection was the binding force, creating warmth and empathy among the members, but leadership was also crucially important; Paul devoted a lot of attention to the choice of leaders and boosted their profile as well as their spiritual resources by such devices as the laying on of hands. The leader filled with the Spirit can be expected to generate in the others the desire to emulate such characteristics as optimism, benevolence, a feeling that life is worthwhile. This is true in secular society, and there is no reason to doubt that the shared meals of the early Christians at their best demonstrated these qualities, especially in the house churches of the first century, where the head of the household presided. Christian commitment was the binding force, but it was also possible for dissension to arise, as it does in associations of various kinds today. To his grief, Paul found that insensitivity in relation to sharing food made food a disruptive factor rather than a constructive one in the Corinthian community.

The Roman context
We have already seen some of the ways in which the celebration of the Eucharist changed over time. In Justin's account, we saw how the coming together of several communities, who had up until then shared the Eucharist in the form of a domestic meal, introduced an element of individual communion, resulting from the larger size of the gatherings and the emergence of permanent roles of service in the community. The evolution of fixed formulas for the Eucharistic Prayer at the centre of the celebration did occur, and the change of

the Church's status under the Emperor Constantine (c. 312) affected not just vestments but also the details of the celebration of the Eucharist. In the Roman Empire of that time,

> the prefects of the city of Rome ... when they made their public procession to their court, had lighted candles and the *Liber Mandarum*, or book of the Emperor's decrees, carried before them.[4]

As the Church took over the basilicas, the court buildings, and built its own churches, the popes adopted the Roman civic rituals when they functioned as magistrates, as Constantine empowered them to do for cases involving clerics.

> This implied that they, and to some extent the presbyters, had to be assigned a corresponding place in the civil hierarchy. Thus the clergy acquired the titles and insignia that state dignitaries enjoyed. Examples of such insignia for bishops, particularly the bishop of Rome, are the imperial *cappa magna*, throne ... and gold ring.[5]

It is worth noting here that up to the Vatican Council, it was customary for bishops to wear the *cappa magna*, the very long cloak with a trainbearer, when entering their cathedrals for mass.

The papal mass

The civic ritual procedure extended to the liturgy. When the pope entered a basilica taken over for liturgical purposes, or the newly built St Peter's, now also called a basilica,[6] he was preceded by a book of the Gospels and seven lighted candles. The rest of his entourage, some bishops from outlying churches, presbyters, and deacons, took the places previously occupied by advocates. The table on which the book of decrees had been placed now became an altar of sacrifice at which the pope stood alone, and no cloths were spread on it until the offertory rite. The altar was in practice a wooden table and wood continued to be used for altars in new churches, but often with decorative panels of precious metals around them, thereby concealing the wood and ceasing to look like a table. There was no simple distinction between a communion table and an altar of sacrifice.[7]

The idea of sharing the eucharistic meal was affected to an extent by the environment created by the disposition of the group: the pope standing alone except when aided by presbyters, the people standing in a group apart. The presbyters flanked the pope from the time of the offertory to hold up large plates (*patenae*) or flask (*ama*) of wine for the eucharistic prayer. This way of celebrating did express what might be called a structured unity and a shared meal, as the bread for the Eucharist consisted of loaves provided by the faithful and collected together on the patens. Their offerings of wine brought by them in small flasks (*amulae*) were used to fill the larger one, which could be large enough to require support by two deacons.

The size of the vessels needed gives a clear indication that all the people present received the Eucharist. The *patenae* for the papal liturgy in the fourth century weighed about 10 kilos, the *ama* ranged in capacity from 15 to 50 litres depending on the size of the congregation, though when Emperor Constantine built St Peter's Basilica, he provided many small chalices and small patens, indicating that individual presbyters concelebrated with the pope, each holding his own vessels.

The social structure of fourth-and-fifth century Rome needs to be taken into account when endeavouring to form an image of the participation of the people in the celebration of the Eucharist. Society was rigidly structured. The nobility were both rich and powerful and were surrounded by a crowd of followers and dependents, known as *clientes*, in effect courtiers, who even escorted them through the streets of Rome and depended on their patronage, their *liberalitas*. There was an upper-middle class, the *equites,* and at the bottom of the social order the *plebs*, numbering tens of thousands, who lived in *insulae,* multi-storey tenements, and supported themselves in labouring jobs or were unemployed. The *plebs* did not benefit directly from the largesse of the nobles but were able to avail of the food distributed free on the authority of successive emperors. For example, already in the third century, the emperor Severus Alexander decreed that ready-baked bread rather than grain should be distributed to the people. Some decades later, the emperor Aurelian 'increased the daily ration to almost one and a half pounds'.[8] The ordinary people were also given the leftovers from the public banquets held after the funerals of their betters.[9]

This rigid structuring of society must have affected a celebration of the Eucharist by the pope; participation by the faithful must have reflected their social status and left the faithful who were part of the *plebs* population last in order for the reception of communion. Given the status of Christianity under Constantine, there may have been many new and uninstructed Christians among the lower classes, who might not have received the Eucharist and would not feel at home in an environment of elaborate liturgy. The better off brought bread for the celebration, and there seems to have been a gradual change from their offering it at the Offertory to an arrangement in which deacons took over and selected the number of loaves to be used. There is also evidence, however, that the people participated by taking part in what is today called the Prayer of the Faithful.[10]

According to a fifth-century document, the bread was that in common use, as a story from the ministry of Pope Gregory the Great (590–604) illustrates. A Roman matron presented herself for communion at a mass celebrated by him, and as he was about to administer the sacrament, she seemed amused (*lasciva*), whereupon he returned the sacrament to the altar. Questioned afterwards why she laughed, she said that she recognised that it was the oblation-loaf she had made with her own hands and found that coincidence amusing.[11]

It would not be surprising if in the conditions described not everyone present actually received the Eucharist, and there is evidence that this was the case. In a treatise attributed to St Ambrose (+ 397), *De Sacramentis,* the newly baptised were urged not to imitate the Greeks, who received just once a year. Among the Greeks, where the liturgy was even more elaborate than in Rome, St John Chrysostom (347–407) of Constantinople did complain: 'In vain we stand before the altar, there is no one to partake'.[12]

Meal and sacrifice

The theology of the mass emphasised in the decrees of the Council of Trent was simply that it was a sacrifice, Christ's propitiatory sacrifice made present. Today we understand that Christ's sacrifice was indeed once and for all, as the Letter to the Hebrews says (7:28), but the celebration of the Paschal Mystery means the offering of Christ's sacrifice of his life is present in the rite along with his restoration, his resurrection. As John Chrysostom emphasised in his day:

> Do not we offer every day? We offer indeed, but making a remembrance of his death, and this (remembrance) is one and not many. How is it one, and not many? Inasmuch as that (sacrifice) was once for all offered, (and) carried into the Holy of Holies. This is a figure of that (sacrifice) and this is a remembrance of that. For we always offer the same, not one sheep now and tomorrow another, but always the same thing: so that the sacrifice is one.[13]

If the Council of Trent's concentration on the truth of the Eucharist as a sacrifice were the only perspective to be considered, with no focus on the Eucharist as a sacrificial meal, there would really be a difficulty for the faithful in comprehending and participating in the Paschal Mystery of Christ's saving work. The difficulty could be stated thus: God the Father appeared to have a role only as the one to whom sacrifice was offered. The Holy Spirit was not mentioned. This difficulty was no longer a problem with the introduction of the idea of our participation in the Paschal Mystery. But the need arises to reconcile the notion of sacrifice, central to the old, with all the new thinking. It is basically a case of reconciling current liturgical thinking with the older concentration on the Eucharist as a sacrament, the sacrament of Christ's presence; it amounts to comparing a dynamic approach with a static one. The older concentration on sacrifice, a theory conveniently labelled Tridentine, did seem to focus on death; the Paschal Mystery approach goes beyond death towards resurrection.

It will be helpful to say more about sacrifice in order to move the focus back to the idea of a meal, even a banquet, in which we receive more than we give. We can ask what the early Christians believed they were doing when celebrating the Eucharist. They came from a long tradition of sacrifice, exemplified by the rites in the Jerusalem Temple. The basic meaning of sacrifice has always been that it involved an offerer, an oblation or object offered and an action directing the oblation to someone, with the intention of achieving some aim.

When that formula, so to speak, is applied to the Christian theological understanding of sacrifice, it becomes very problematic, for even in the Old Testament, there are plenty of texts to indicate the irrelevance, the emptiness of ritual offerings of objects or animals to God.[14] Further, can God need anything that Christians can do for him? But if the initiative is not ours but God's, a new understanding of the Eucharist as sacrifice emerges. Present-day thinking has taken the radical step of changing God the Father's role from that which was at the heart of the Tridentine understanding of the sacrifice of the mass: God the Father having a role only as the one to whom sacrifice was offered. The new understanding, really that recovered from the patristic era, was well articulated in a book by Edward Kilmartin SJ, *The Eucharist in the West*, published posthumously in 1998:

> Sacrifice is not in the first place an activity of human beings directed to God and, in the second place, something that reaches its goal in the response of divine acceptance and bestowal of divine blessing on the cultic community. Rather, sacrifice in the New Testament understanding – and thus in its Christian understanding – is in the first place, the self-offering of the Father in the gift of his Son, and in the second place the unique response of the Son in his humanity to the Father, and in the third place the self-offering of believers in

union with Christ by which they share in his covenant relation with the Father.

To harmonise the previously customary doctrine about sacrifice with what is central to consideration of the Mystery of Christ and our participation in it, it may be helpful to recall the motivations for offering mentioned at the beginning of this chapter. The term 'Eucharist' is the key. What we offer at mass is thanksgiving, thanksgiving for Christ's saving work, carried out in accordance with the Father's will to save his people and made present as the Paschal Mystery, through the power of the Spirit. That motive of thanksgiving, which emphasises the idea of celebration and is appropriately done in the form of a meal, does not exclude other motivations consistent with the Paschal Mystery. The motive of self-offering, of sharing in Christ's sufferings, follows from the fact of the people being the Body of Christ. But a balance is required; Christ saved us, we do not save ourselves, a point by chance well made in the novel *Chocolat*.

It is a story centred on the conflict between the Curé, Reynaud, and Vianne Rocher, who opened a *chocolaterie* opposite his church on Ash Wednesday and proceeded to upset the staid pattern of life of the villagers by her tempting chocolate confections. The struggle, much of it from a distance, is of epic proportions and is presented by the author as a love of life on the woman's part and a loveless, death-wishing spirituality on the part of the Curé, the Black Man. There is a revealing soliloquy by the Curé at one point, as he struggles throughout Lent to keep up his rigorous fast, undertaking increasing hardship as a spiritual weapon against this 'witch', who he believes is out to destroy both him and his parish:

> I wonder how many of them have already broken their Lenten promises … For myself, I feel that fasting cleanses me. The mere sight of the butcher's window appals; odours are heightened to a point of intensity that makes my head reel. Suddenly, the morning odour from Poitou's bakery is more than I can bear. I myself have touched neither meat nor fish nor

eggs for over a week ... and I am cleansed. I only wish I could do more. This is not suffering. This is not penance. I sometimes feel that if I could only show them the right example, if it could be me on that cross bleeding, suffering.[15]

The Curé seems to think that his sacrifices have a pivotal role in making Christ's sacrifice effective in the lives of his parishioners. He could say, 'In my own body I do what I can to make up all that has still to be undergone by Christ for the sake of his body, the Church' (Col 1:24), but what this means is that those who suffer in this world are privileged participants in the eternal act which Christ accomplished in history by undergoing the sufferings of his passion as the necessary means of returning to the Father from this world. The truth is, whether it is Reynaud or ourselves, 'We must share his sufferings if we are to share his glory' (Cf. Rom 8:17). This we can do in many ways in daily life, but the most profound way we, personally and as members of the Body of Christ, share in his sufferings is by participating with deep faith and hope and love in the Paschal Mystery during the celebration of the Eucharist. Doing so, we are assured that this leads to sharing in his resurrection in the form of a new life, even here in the present world. It is telling that this theology of sacrifice does away with any notion of sacrifice in which human beings take the initiative or bargain with God.

This move of the initiative back to God can be difficult to accept for people who believe it is natural and proper to initiate acts of worship of God. It seems natural to take the initiative, to approach God offering something and expecting to get something in return, just as primitive peoples made offerings to the fertility gods in order to ensure a good harvest, an attitude nicely summed up in the Latin tag: *do ut des* – I give so that you may give. But the teaching of *Sacrosanctum Concilium* gives priority not to human initiative but to God's gift of the sanctification of those who celebrate the liturgy of the Church; it gives priority to the downward movement of grace, over the upward movement of the Church's act of praise and thanksgiving.[16]

From that perspective, seeing the rite of the Eucharist as a celebratory meal of thanksgiving makes sense in a way that is consistent with the idea of the 'sacrifice of the mass', the traditional term. The compatibility of the two perspectives is apparent in the Eastern celebration of the Eucharist. In the Liturgy of Basil the Great, used ten times a year in the Greek-speaking Church, a hymn sung on Holy Saturday during the Great Entrance (the Offertory rite) has the sacrificial theme of Christ going to be slain but also that of a meal:

> Let all mortal flesh be silent, and stand in fear and trembling and harbour no earthly thoughts; for the King of Kings and Lord of Lords is entering to be slain and given as food to the faithful.[17]

The reference to Christ being slain and given as food while the bread and wine are being carried in procession, shows that the Eastern liturgy has had from earliest times a sense of sacrifice and of its commemoration in a meal.

Animal sacrifice

It is not therefore surprising that in addition to the 'breaking of the bread' tradition, early Christians in some places took this link between a sacrificial death and food to the level of imitating its Jewish origins in the Feast of Pasch. They engaged in a rite of animal sacrifice, though now with the intention of making an offering to the God of the Christians. The evidence for this comes largely from the area in which Orthodox rather than Western Christianity predominates. It is likely that early Christians had a difficulty in finding meat for their consumption that was not the product of a pagan sacrifice, 'offered to idols', as Paul recognised in 1 Corinthians 10:23–30. The universal availability of meat from sacrifices can be explained by the fact that

> the Greeks never failed to maintain relations with the divine powers through the ritualised killing of animal victims,

whose flesh was consumed collectively according to precise strictures.[18]

A way around the difficulty for Christians could have been to find animals for themselves and slaughter them as an offering to the true God. This may be the explanation for what happened in various places. There is evidence that in Armenia, at least, Christians continued to offer sacrifice to God through animal slaughter and a subsequent meal, and there is documentary evidence from the early fifth century, from the twelfth and even from the early twentieth century for the continuation of this practice in Armenia.[19]

In the early twentieth century, an Anglican missionary and medical doctor concerned with the welfare of Syrian villagers, Archdeacon McLean, gave an account of his experiences in a small area where Turkey and Syria meet. He witnessed the slaughter of sheep as an offering to God, but not considered a propitiatory sacrifice by these Armenian Christians or as 'supplementing the sacrifice of Calvary'.[20] The original name for the victim, *matal*, has given way in modern Armenian liturgical practice to *matagh*, and the ceremony is prominently associated with commemorating the Armenian massacre of 1915.

The persistence of the 'sanctified slaughter' of animals in Greece was chronicled in an article in 1979, which made it clear that these sacrifices are offered outside the church building, usually after the celebration of the liturgy, and are associated with particular feast days, such as that of St Elias (20 July) and St Athanasius (18 January).[21] After the slaughter, participants dipped a finger in the blood and made the sign of the cross. Before the meal, the priest or bishop blessed the meat while it was stewing with various herbs and vegetables in a cauldron.[22] Clearly, such a celebration augments the experience of festivity on the feast day and adds a sacral character to what in other contemporary cultures would simply be a case of a religious feast being used as the *occasion* for a festive meal.

In the early 1990s, the writer William Dalrymple encountered the practice of animal sacrifice during a visit to the ruined town of

Cyrrhus, forty-five miles north of Aleppo in Syria. A small mosque dating from the thirteenth or fourteenth century housed the shrine of a Sufi saint, named Nebi Uri, perhaps confusedly identified with Uriah the Hittite, who is honoured as a saint by Muslims, as his story is told in both the Quran and the Bible (2 Sam 11 and 12). The guardian told the writer that many Christians as well as Muslims came regularly to the shrine, many seeking healing.[23] Dalrymple encountered a similar practice at the shrine of St George at Beit Jala in the Christian quarter of Jerusalem. The Greek Orthodox custodian, Fr Methodius, told him that as many Muslims as Christians came there with their offerings, including sheep, which – in his own words – he sacrificed, keeping only a small portion for himself, while the rest went to the poor.[24]

Adverting to the idea of animal sacrifice links the Christian celebration of the Eucharist with the Feast of Pasch of Jewish history, but also establishes a connection with Jesus' act of replacing the Old Covenant with the New by the sacrifice of his own life.

Conclusion

In this chapter, I have endeavoured to show that while the people can be considered to be participating in, or offering, a sacrifice because of the deeply embedded traditional way the mass was described, the fact that the celebration involves food and drink makes the idea of a meal clearly relevant. When the mass is considered a celebration of the Paschal Mystery, the importance of the meal dimension of the celebration becomes abundantly clear.

Endnotes

1. Geraldine Mostère, 'Experience, Subjectivity and Performance', in *Understanding Religious Rituals: Theoretical Approaches and Innovations*, ed by John P. Hoffmann (Abingdon, Oxon: Routledge, 2012), 54–72. Liam Tracey, 'Liturgical Studies in a New Millennium', *Irish Theological Quarterly*, 66 (2001), p. 349: 'As liturgists we have to admit that we have not reflected sufficiently on what people actually experience Sunday after Sunday, the meaning(s) they attribute to that practice individually and collectively.'
2. Pope John Paul II, *Ecclesia de Eucharistia* (Vatican: The Holy See, 2003), 10.

3. Robert Disch, *The Ecological Conscience: Values for Survival* (Upper Saddle River, NJ: Prentice Hall, 1970), p. 96.
4. *Ordo Romanus Primus*, with introduction and notes by E. G. Cuthbert, F. Atchley (London: The De La More Press, 1905), p. 9.
5. Ansgar Chupungco, 'History of the Liturgy until the Fourth Century', pp. 108–9.
6. *Ordo Romanus Primus*, p. 10.
7. *A Dictionary of Liturgy and Worship*, p. 4.
8. Reay Tannahill, *Food in History* (London: Headline Publishing, 1998), p. 71.
9. Veronika Grimm, *From Feasting to Fasting: The Evolution of a Sin* (London: Routledge, 1996), p. 39.
10. Paul de Clerk, *The 'Universal Prayer'*.
11. The story is found in John the Deacon, *Vita sancti Gregorii papae*, lib. II, cap. 41, reproduced in Gregory the Great, *Sancti Gregorii Papae I, Cognomento Magni, Opera Omnia* (Paris: J. P. Migne, 1862), Col. 549.
12. Chrysostom, 'Homily on the Epistle to the Ephesians', in *Commentary on the Epistle to the Galatians and Homilies on the Epistles to the Ephesians* (London: J. G. F. and J. Rivington,1840), 3.4, p. 132.
13. Chrysostom, 'Homily on Hebrews', in 'Homilies on the Gospel of St John and the Epistle to the Hebrews', *Nicene and Post-Nicene Fathers*, vol. XIV (Grand Rapids: Eerdmans, 1956), 17.6, p. 459.
14. See, for example, Psalm 40, verse 6: 'Sacrifice and offering you do not desire, but you have given me an open ear. Burnt offering and sin offering you have not required.'
15. Joanne Harris, *Chocolat* (Waterville, Maine: Thorndike Press, 1999) pp. 88–89.
16. *Sacrosanctum Concilium*, 7.
17. Hans-Joachim Schultz, *The Byzantine Liturgy*, trans. by Matthew J. O'Connell (New York: Pueblo, 1986), p. 37.
18. Andrew McGowan, *Ascetic Eucharists: Food and Drink in Early Christian Ritual Meals* (Oxford: Clarendon Press, 1999), pp. 60–1.
19. The early evidence comes from the *Armenian Canons of St (Isaak) Sahak* (354–439).
20. Frederick C. Conybeare, 'The Survival of Animal Sacrifices inside the Christian Church', in *The American Journal of Theology*, 7:1 (January 1903), 62–90.
21. Stella Georgoudi, '*L'égorgement sanctifié en Grece moderne*', in *La Cuisinne du Sacrifice en Pays Grec*, ed by Marcel Detienne et Jean-Pierre Vernant (Paris: Editions Gallimard, 1979), p. 279.
22. Georgoudi, '*L'égorgement sanctifié*', p. 284.
23. William Dalrymple, *From the Holy Mountain: A Journey in the Shadow of Byzantium* (London: HarperCollins, 1997), pp. 166–9.
24. Dalrymple, *From the Holy Mountain*, p. 339.

4: How Can the People Express Their Eucharistic Belief?

In chapter three, I showed that the celebration of the Eucharist can be understood as a sacrifice, as tradition has emphasised, but also as a meal. In either case, belief is in the presence of the risen Christ is central. As will be seen below, a fundamental issue over the centuries since the end of the first millennium has been how to express that belief.

Belief that the celebration of the Eucharist brings about Christ's presence was at least implicit in the early days of the 'breaking of the bread', as described in chapter two. That the bread and wine were changed into the body and blood of Christ was asserted by Justin in the second century. Justin had used the word 'transmutation'; Gregory of Nyssa, in the fourth century, talked of 'trans-elementation', while Cyril of Jerusalem, in his 'Catechetical Lecture 23', about the same time, said the bread was 'made' into the body of Christ. Augustine, in the fifth century, said that it received Christ's blessing, and that 'it becomes the body of Christ', but in fact he used the simple expression that the sacrament of Christ's body is 'in a certain way' the body of Christ, and the sacrament of his blood 'in a certain way' the blood of Christ.[1] Augustine had left a somewhat ambiguous legacy to the sacramental theology of the future, as he used both the figurative and the realist approach in different parts of his works.[2] Modern scholarship would hold that these early theologians, despite their realistic language, favoured a more spiritual than localised presence of Christ.

Looking back to the celebrations of the Eucharist of the early centuries, we find that an important development occurred in relation to the Eucharistic Prayer at the centre of the celebration. There was a gradual evolution of fixed formulas compared with the presider's freedom in formulating prayer in Justin's time. The growing importance of the papacy from the fourth century onwards, and its authority in relation to the liturgy, made the emergence over a period of the Eucharistic Prayer called the Roman Canon (now Eucharistic Prayer I) a significant event. Making Christ's own words, 'This is my body, this is my blood' essential for an authentic celebration, as became the case in the West by the time of Ambrose (339–397)[3] in the late fourth century, had a decisive effect on the understanding of the Eucharist in later centuries.

The Middle Ages

The new Emperor of the West, Charlemagne (742–814), relied on receiving liturgical books from Rome, and this helped to shape the form of the celebration for the West generally. It was a time of largely unquestioning attitudes regarding what was happening in the celebration and of concentration on the *experience* of liturgical ceremony, which Charlemagne thoroughly enjoyed. There are reasons why this unenquiring attitude obtained. Since the early centuries, when both Eastern and Western fathers of the Church had reflected on the mystery of the Eucharist, experience was predominant rather than speculation, and there were centuries when the breakdown of civilisation left little opportunity for scholarly investigation.

By the time of Charlemagne's grandson, Charles the Bald (823–877), Saxon tribes were being Christianised and integrated into the Frankish kingdom, with the result that the programme of catechising them raised questions that up to then had not needed to be faced.

In particular, how could a ritual involving common, coarse bread make Christ present? (For such people, accustomed to beer, wine was recognised as special.) In response to questions received from some 'young' Churches, a monk of Corbie, Paschasius Radbertus (785–865), relied on texts by second-century Irenaeus and fourth-century Hilary of Poitiers to set out as plainly as he could the teaching of the Church on the Eucharist. Charles the Bald considered Paschasius's theory an overly material concept of Christ's body – that Christ was present in a material and not simply in some spiritual way, as had been the common understanding. This caused controversy to begin between theologians about how Christ was present in the Eucharist. The attempt to provide a rational expression for what is essentially a mystery lasted several centuries. But even as this speculation became widespread, developments in liturgical *practice* also influenced thinking.

It is important to draw attention to a development in relation to the bread of the Eucharist in the late eighth century and ninth century, perhaps in reaction to the coarse quality of what was generally available. The introduction of the small, round, white wafer of unleavened bread would take several centuries to become standard, but the use of the white wafer supported the view that bread was no longer there but transformed into Christ's body, making Christ in some way visible. That view led to the practice of the adoration of the Eucharist in a monstrance. Clearly, a white wafer, less liable to fragmentation because unleavened, made this more feasible, but the fact that it was now called the 'host' was indicative of the emphasis on the sacrificial nature of Christ's presence, as the word in its Latin version, *hostia*, means 'victim'. The use of unleavened bread would also serve to bring into relief the origin of the Eucharist in the Last Supper, when the Lord celebrated with his disciples, using unleavened bread as the Jewish rite required. But this departure from the appearance of bread had the effect of lessening the sense of food as medieval people, who were accustomed to coarse bread, would have understood it. With it came a new reverence on the part of the laity, a reluctance to consume what was now the focus of adoration.

By the eleventh century, when devotion to the eucharistic host had become so marked, the making of the bread in some places took on a liturgical format. According to the customs of the Abbey of Hirsau in Germany, the wheat had to be selected kernel by kernel, and there were ceremonies surrounding the milling with a machine that had been cleaned and hung about with curtains. The four monks who baked the bread had to wear liturgical vestments and three of them had to be deacons or priests.[4]

It is understandable that if such a reverential approach to the making of the hosts obtained, the attitude of the laity must have been one of awe and fear when the host was changed into the body of Christ. To such an extent did this attitude of reverential fear prevail that the Fourth Lateran Council in 1215 had to rule that the faithful were bound to confess their sins and receive communion at least once a year. A historian, Caroline Bynum, summed up the situation:

> By the thirteenth century, the Eucharist, once a communal meal that bound Christians together and fed them with the comfort of heaven, had become an object of adoration.[5]

New thinking

The period from the ninth to the thirteenth century saw a new flourishing of creative thinking; theological reflection on the Eucharist would become a dominant feature of the Church's life. This reflection would be polarised into, on the one hand, an attitude that considered Christ's presence to be figurative, as Augustine had once put it, meaning spiritual but not physical, and on the other, a localised or physical presence, what is in English called 'the real presence', a direct translation of the Latin term in use at the time: *presentia realis*. The Latin *realis* is the adjectival form of *in re*, presence in a thing, which is a very strong term; Christ's presence can be seen as a material thing, and in fact in the course of the controversy that broke out – between monk theologians initially – that very materialistic view was held by some.

An unfortunate French logician and theologian, Berengarius (999–1088), who held a very spiritual view of Christ's presence because of his logical analysis of Christ's words, was forced at a synod in Rome in 1059 to subscribe to an oath containing the words:

> I believe that the bread and wine, which are placed on the altar, are after consecration not only a sacrament but also the true body and blood of our Lord Jesus Christ, and with the senses not only sacramentally but in truth are taken and broken by the hands of the priests and crushed by the teeth of the faithful.[6]

There were theologians who defended the bizarre nature of this theory by saying that as Christ was God he did not suffer in the course of mastication.

Berengarius repudiated the vow on his return soon afterwards to France. It was soon clear to most theologians of the time that this grossly stated formula was an error. Efforts were made to find a new approach. Berengarius was required to take a new oath at a synod in Rome in 1079, where the distinction between substance and accidents was employed to defend the 'realist' position. 'Substance' comes from the Latin, *substans*, standing underneath, the reality underneath the appearance, the accidents. This basically philosophical approach was gaining ground to defend the real presence theory, even though there was the problem of how the appearance, even the weight etc., of the bread could have some kind of suspended existence in the air, when the substance of the bread was replaced by the substance of Christ's body.

A decisive moment came when the Fourth Lateran Council in 1215 decreed that the presence of Christ came about through transubstantiation, a term used by a French bishop in the eleventh-century, though what the Council meant by that was not clear (to the Council or to others!), and theologians for several centuries debated how it was to be interpreted. One meaning was that after the recitation of the words of Christ during the celebration, the bread and wine remained, but the body and blood of Christ became present also.[7] Another view was that the bread and wine were completely annihilated, and only the body and blood of Christ remained. But if this is the case, what from the point of view of the person receiving the Eucharist was happening? The sensation in the mouth of consuming could only be a phantasm. Over time, the view prevailed that the substance of the bread was changed into the substance of the body of Christ and similarly with the wine, with the appearances of bread and wine somehow remaining.

When the medieval theory of Christ's body being eaten physically and his blood drunk had given way to the theology of substantial change (transubstantiation), the question arose whether the words had to be spoken separately over the two elements in order to bring about Christ's presence. Theologians in the Sorbonne University, in about 1198, decided that the formula pronounced over the bread resulted in the presence of the whole Christ, body, blood, soul and divinity – the same would be true in relation to the wine. This justified the reception of the Eucharist under the appearance of bread only, and that practice became normative, and a further step away from what Christ instituted and from the idea of a shared meal.

The Council of Trent

As is well known, Thomas Aquinas opted for the transubstantiation view, basing it on the philosophy of Aristotle, though he held on to the idea of the Eucharist being food in his famous hymn *Adoro te*, describing the Eucharist as *panis vivus* (living bread to mortals life supplying). It is important to realise that theologians held diverse views for centuries about the Eucharist, and it was only at the Council of Trent, which saw arguments among theologians favouring one view or other, that the doctrine was defined in accordance with Aquinas's theory, though the term used was conversion, *conversio*.

> The holy council now declares ... that by the consecration of the bread and wine a change (*conversio*) is brought about of the whole substance of the bread into the substance of the body of Christ our Lord, and of the whole substance of the wine into the substance of his blood.

The Decree added:

> This change the holy Catholic Church properly and appropriately calls transubstantiation.[9]

There has been much debate, especially since Vatican II, regarding the theological status of transubstantiation, a philosophical theory, but it is worth noting that in the early Christian centuries articulating the Church's belief concerning Jesus – his human and divine natures – involved using the terminology of Greek philosophy.

A consequence of all this development is that the ideas of celebration and of the Eucharist as food have given way to consideration of the doctrine of the Eucharist in itself, with no obvious connection with celebration or participation by the people, except in relation to individual reception of the Eucharist. From the perspective of the history of the theology of the Eucharistic celebration, that brings us effectively to the present.

One consequence is that the false tension between the sacrificial and meal dimensions of the Eucharist surfaces quite easily for those who are strongly attached to traditional eucharistic theology. Pope St John Paul could say in 2003, 'Christ remains with us in the Eucharist, making his presence in meal and sacrifice the promise of a humanity renewed by his love'.[10] Yet, as noted in the previous chapter, he also expressed concern that some approaches to the Eucharist result in its being 'celebrated as if it were simply a fraternal banquet'.[11]

Lessons from the East

A different atmosphere prevails in the eucharistic celebration of the Churches of the East, Greek Orthodox and others. The Eastern tradition did not follow the Western path of applying categories of philosophical thought *a priori* to the Eucharist, but developed its reflection on the mystery from the lived *experience* of the Church and recognised the limits of rational thought in face of mystery. The 'lived experience' centres on material elements, bread and wine, causing the words 'Christian materialism' to appear in Orthodox writings. As the Orthodox theologian, Andrew Louth, noted:

> (R)unning through the history of the Church there has been a constant struggle against a tendency towards a false spiritualisation, that opposes the spiritual to the material, and seeks flight from the material.[12]

That comment brings to mind the medieval Western development of the round white host replacing ordinary bread and the rituals that resulted. Eastern reflection, on the other hand, places great emphasis on the continuing importance of the material elements in making Christ present in the celebration. As the theologian, Kallistos Ware, pointed out, the Orthodox Church takes material things and makes them a vehicle of the Spirit:

> Orthodoxy rejects any attempt to diminish the materiality of the sacraments, the human person is to be seen in holistic terms, as an integral unity of soul and body, and so the sacramental worship in which we humans participate should involve to the full our bodies along with our minds. ... At the Eucharist, leavened bread is used, not just wafers.[13]

Symbolism is prominent in the architecture and decoration of Orthodox churches. A pervading scent of incense, votive lamps, characteristically beautiful chant, icons on walls and iconostasis (icon screen) already create an atmosphere of mystery, notably so because of the closing off of the sanctuary from the place of the assembly of the faithful. In the context of the people's celebration, the liturgy has to be seen as a clerical performance, hidden from the eyes of the faithful for most of the long duration of the service, yet, as will be seen below, the people do have a profound sense of participation.

In general, the Orthodox Eucharist exhibits a sacrificial character, especially as the bread of offering is prepared by making an incision in the form of a cross with a lance, while the priest says, in the Greek rite, 'Like a lamb he was led to sacrifice, and was silent like a little lamb before its shearers.' The texts used represent not so much the death on the cross – the primary signification of the action of the priest – as the Old Testament slaughter of the paschal lamb and, above all, the incarnation and the birth of Christ.

From the perspective of now customary Western practice, the eucharistic liturgy does not obviously present as a meal or banquet, as it is lacks a tradition of regular communion by the faithful. At the conclusion of the liturgy, there is a custom of giving them small pieces cut from the bread prepared for the offering at a table behind the icon screen. In the Russian Orthodox tradition, these pieces, along with un-consecrated wine, are sometimes given to communicants immediately after they have actually received the consecrated elements – as a way, it would seem, of linking participation in the sacrifice with sharing in a meal.

Much of the ceremony is hidden from the people behind the icon screen and a choir traditionally provides the chant, yet worshippers experience a strong sense of participation at some special moments, for example, when a cleric emerges from the mystery-filled ceremony within the sanctuary and silently incenses the people before returning there once more. The faithful already experience a heightened sense of participation when it is time for what in the Western liturgy is called the Offertory Procession. At this point, the Great Entrance takes place. It has always been a very significant rite, and the people are closely involved. The gifts are brought in procession out through the north door in the icon screen and then carried in solemnly by one of the priests through the assembly before entering the sanctuary through the other door in the icon screen.

> As the procession appears the people cross themselves and bow, and many may kneel and prostrate themselves as the richly veiled chalice and paten are carried past.[14]

This suggests that for the faithful the symbolising function of the bread and wine is already operative, that Christ is already present in mystery. In effect, the faithful have a heightened sense of celebrating the Paschal Mystery. One fifth-century interpretation of the rite saw the placing of the bread on the altar as laying the dead Christ in the tomb, soon to be raised during the Eucharistic Prayer.[15]

Through the centuries, the Great Entrance has represented for the people various aspects of the mystery of Christ's life and work: Christ being led away to his passion, the revelation of the hidden mystery of salvation, his journey to Jerusalem on Palm Sunday and even the final coming of Christ. This multi-faceted symbolic and representational approach to the celebration, relying on movement as much as on the text of the hymns, and involving a richly ornamented cover for chalice and paten, and ornate vestments for the priest, enables the worshippers to experience a sense of mystery and be drawn into it in a way which is unique to the Eastern world.

Reservation of the Eucharist
Reservation of the Eucharist for the communion of the sick has always been in a container called the ark, often shaped like a boat, and not visible behind the icon screen. There is therefore no tradition of exposition of the sacrament; Orthodox theology has not focused on eucharistic adoration as happened in the West, because the doctrine of the sacraments in relation to the Eucharist has avoided any suggestion of a physical presence. It considers the elements of bread and wine to be symbols of the body and blood of Christ, where 'symbol' has a profound meaning, one that is very different from that implied when the term 'mere symbol' is used.

This understanding of symbol has been articulated comprehensively by the Orthodox theologian, Alexander Schememann, who emphasised that while bread and wine are suitable in a superficially symbolical way to represent body and blood, their symbolism runs much deeper than being an 'illustration':

> (T)his is precisely the heart of the matter: the primary meaning of symbol is in no way equivalent to illustration. In fact it is possible for the symbol *not* to illustrate, that is, it can

be devoid of any similarity with that which it symbolises ... This is because the purpose and function of the symbol is *not* to illustrate (this would presume the *absence* of what is illustrated) but to *manifest* and to *communicate* what is manifested. We might say that the symbol does not so much 'resemble' the reality that it symbolises as it *participates* in it, and therefore it is capable of communicating it in reality ... (I)n the original understanding it is the manifestation and presence of the *other* reality – but precisely as *other*, which, under given circumstances cannot be manifested and made present in any other way than as symbol.[16]

Contemporary issues in the West

Even before Vatican II, some Western theologians had sought to reflect on the mystery of the eucharistic celebration in terms of experience, recognising that the words and actions and material elements have a symbolic value beyond the immediate perception of sound or touch. 'Symbolic' can often have a superficial connotation, but in itself has the profound significance of being a gateway to a reality beyond itself.

The words of the eucharistic rite have a performative and not just a narrative function, they manifest the reality of the Paschal Mystery. At a certain point, the material bread and wine bring access to communion with the risen Jesus. In the discussion of the liturgy at Vatican II, the theology of the Paschal Mystery influenced the way the presence of Christ was described – in the Eucharist itself, in the presider, in the Word and in the 'nonordained' as members of the Body of Christ. There were objections to this fourfold presence, out of fear that Christ's presence in the eucharistic species might be 'belittled'. The text was approved by 2049 votes as against 66. The commentator on the text, Josef Jungmann, made the point:

> The resistance evidently sprang from a theological school of thought little accustomed to conceiving the continued

existence of the Lord in his transfigured humanity in the glory of the Father as his primary manner of being, which operates fully in all other modes of his presence, even though in different ways.[17]

That comment amounts to the very critical judgment that those bishops who opposed the text did not take account of Paschal Mystery theology, the foundation of the constitution.

Two months before the conclusion of the Council in 1965, Pope Paul VI issued an encyclical, *Mysterium Fidei,* in which he reacted against the literature that had emerged on the concept of symbolism as a way of expressing the theology of the Eucharist. He acknowledged that 'the Fathers and the (medieval) Scholastics had a great deal to say about symbolism in the Eucharist',[18] but stated:

> While eucharistic symbolism is well suited to helping us understand the effect that is proper to this sacrament – the unity of the Mystical Body – still it does not indicate or explain what it is that makes this sacrament different from all the others.[19]

This reservation about symbolism underlies the *Credo of the People of God,*[20] issued by the Pope in 1968, In the *Credo* it is stated that

> Every theological explanation which seeks some understanding of this mystery must, in order to be in accord with Catholic faith, maintain that in the reality itself, independently of our mind, the bread and wine have ceased to exist after the Consecration, so that it is the adorable body and blood of the Lord Jesus that from then on are really before us under the sacramental species of bread and wine.[21]

As noted earlier in this chapter, one of the medieval theories concerning the Eucharist was the same as that in the *Credo,* that the bread and wine disappeared completely after the consecration, but the Council of Trent effectively rejected that theory.

There is a tendency on the part of both presiders and faithful to consider that part of the liturgy where the words of Christ are used, 'This is my body', 'This is my blood', as marking the moment where the whole mystery of salvation becomes present. The calling down of the Spirit on the gifts is seen as having a new effectiveness in Christ's saving presence. In fact, the celebration of the Paschal Mystery has been in train since the beginning of the celebration and the invocation of the Spirit, since the time of Chrysostom in the fourth century, seen as a calling down of the Spirit on the community as well as on the gifts.[22] It marks the point where the words of Christ and invocation of the Spirit enable the symbolic function of the material elements to effect a union between the participants and the heart of the Paschal Mystery, making the body and blood of the *risen* Christ available to the believer as food. Theodore of Mopsuestia (350–428) expressed this in his own way, saying how in the celebration of the Paschal Mystery the transformation of Christ's body in the resurrection led to a change in the elements:

> In this same way, after the Holy Spirit has come here also, we believe that the elements of bread and wine have received a kind of anointing from the grace that comes upon them, and we hold them to be henceforth immortal, incorruptible, impassible and immutable by nature, as the body of the Lord was after the resurrection.[23]

In a sermon to the newly baptised, Augustine evoked Paul's statement, 'Because there is one bread, we who are many are one body, for we partake of the one bread' (1 Cor 10:27).

> You hear the words, 'the body of Christ' and you reply 'Amen'. Be then a member of Christ's body, so that your 'Amen' may accord with the truth ... Be then what you see, and receive what you are.

He concluded:

> When you were baptised, the Holy Spirit came into you like the fire that bakes the dough. Be then what you see, and receive what you are.[24]

These are complementary approaches, to the point where the celebration of the Paschal Mystery brings, by the power of the Holy Spirit, the earthly and heavenly liturgies into full communion with each other and leads to bodily communion of the believer with Christ. The exchange: 'Lift up your hearts' / 'We have lifted them up to the Lord' has had its fulfilment.[25] Both the Western and Orthodox traditions agree that the combination of the calling down of the Holy Spirit and the words of Christ bring the celebration to that point. Bearing in mind the history of the relationship between the elements and Christ's body and blood from the early centuries until now, this is a safe way to interpret these sacred moments.

To make the *elevation* of the host and chalice the climax of the celebration is to fail to recognise that from the beginning of the rite Christ's saving activity, the Paschal Mystery, is present and indeed through the power of the Spirit. The practice of showing the elements to the people was sanctioned by the Synod of Paris in 1204. This led to the actual climax of the Eucharistic Prayer, 'Through him and with him ... ', to be reduced in significance, whereas it is the point where the community should, as in Justin's day, express its wholehearted participation and thanksgiving for our salvation, with a great 'Amen'.

The renewal of the rite after the Vatican Council restored communion under both kinds as the norm where that was possible. Obviously there can be difficulties here and therefore in implementing the concept of a shared meal, but unity with one another is an integral part of the union with Christ, as Paul had said to the Corinthians (1 Cor 10:16):

> The cup of blessing that we bless, is it not a participation in the blood of Christ? The bread that we break, is it not a

participation in the body of Christ? Because the loaf of bread is one, we, though many, are one body, for we all partake of the one loaf.

For many practising Catholics, there is probably little awareness of a tension between the sacrificial and shared meal dimensions. Rather people hold on to the belief in Christ's presence in the Eucharist learned in childhood, knowing there is such a word as 'transubstantiation' that somehow illuminates the mystery, but which is far too recondite a term to be given further thought. James Joyce, in *Portrait of the Artist as a Young Man*, may well have been expressing his own sentiments in the following exchange:

> 'Do you believe in the Eucharist?', Cranley asked. 'I do not', Stephen said. 'Do you disbelieve, then?', 'I neither believe in it or disbelieve in it', Stephen answered.[26]

That agnostic statement by Stephen Daedalus of neither believing nor disbelieving may well have expressed an attitude beginning to take hold among educated Catholics at a time when the Catholic subculture came up against the secularising forces of twentieth-century modern culture. It might be regarded as reluctance to engage thoughtfully with the mystery of Christ's presence in the Eucharist, but it might also be explained as honest puzzlement, when in modern times medieval philosophy began to appear irrelevant. People were then, and many are now – two generations after the Vatican Council – unaware that a very different way of thinking exists, taken from Scripture, about the eucharistic mystery. The teaching of the Vatican Council about the Paschal Mystery has been in the *Catechism of the Catholic Church* since it appeared in various languages towards the end of the 1990s. It might be expected to have influenced the catechising of the young in the twenty-five years or so since then and be part of mainstream thinking about the Eucharist. That does not seem to be the case, however. An opportunity has been missed to give the faithful who still participate in the celebration of the Eucharist the legitimate satisfaction of participating in depth as the rite unfolds.

Conclusion

The reservation expressed by the minority at the Vatican Council, with regard to the majority's approach to the doctrine of the Eucharist, was an indication of a deep-seated ambivalence on their part about the apparent novelty of making Paschal Mystery theology the foundation of the celebration. Among today's faithful, it would not be surprising if a similar hesitation existed, leaving some alienated from the present liturgical norms and preferring the former 'Latin Mass'. Others who regularly attend may be presumed to have faith, simple or more nuanced, that they have a real encounter with Jesus through the current way of celebrating, while occasional participants may not know what to think and simply act with some degree of reverence when they attend. In pastoral practice, parish clergy – and bishops – may feel that a catechetical programme of instruction on the Eucharist over a period of Sundays (as occurred in the now rather remote past) would not be effective. It would not in any case be in accordance with the homiletic programme required by the renewal of the liturgy.

As Sunday attendances remain small and many continue to feel it sufficient to watch mass online, with consequent reduced numbers actually being fed at the table of the Lord, a great unifying force, a community building resource, is not availed of. The possible approaches to rectifying the situation will be the subject of the final chapter.

Endnotes

1. Augustine, *Letters*, vol. II (Washington DC: Catholic University America Press, 1966), 83–130.
2. See Pamela Jackson, 'Eucharist', in *Augustine Through the Ages: An Encyclopedia*, ed by Allan D. Fitzgerald (Grand Rapids: William B. Eerdmans, 1992), pp. 332–3.
3. Ambrose, *De Mysteriis*, 9.52, 'That sacrament which you receive is made what it is by the word of Christ.'
4. Joseph Jungmann, *The Mass of the Roman Rite: Its Origins and Development*, trans. by F. A. Brunner (London: Burns & Oates, 1959), pp. 330–1.

5. Caroline Bynum, *Holy Feast and Holy Fast*, p. 53.
6. *Enchiridion Symbolorum, Definitionum et Declarationum*, ed by H. Denzinger, A. Schoenmetzer (Freiburg: Herder, 1965), p. 690.
7. Martin Luther subscribed tenaciously to this view until his death in 1546.
8. As is well known, Thomas Aquinas opted for the transubstantiation view, basing it on the philosophy of Aristotle, though he held on to the idea of the Eucharist being food in his famous hymn *Adoro te*, describing the Eucharist as *panis vivus* (living bread to mortals life supplying).
9. Council of Trent, 'Session XIII', October 1551.
10. Pope John Paul II, *Ecclesia de Eucharistia*, 20.
11. Pope John Paul II, *Ecclesia de Eucharistia*, 20.
12. Andrew Louth, *Introducing Eastern Orthodox Theology* (London: SPCK, 2013), p. 98.
13. Timothy Ware, *The Orthodox Church* (London: Penguin Books, 1993, second ed.), pp. 274–5.
14. Hugh Wybrew, *The Orthodox Liturgy: The Development of the Eucharistic Liturgy in the Byzantine Rite* (London: SPCK, 1989), p. 7.
15. Wybrew, *Orthodox Liturgy*, p. 53.
16. Alexander Schmemann, *The Eucharist* (Crestwood, NY: St Vladimir's Seminary Press, 1987), p. 38.
17. Josef Jungmann SJ, 'Constitution on Liturgy', in *Commentary on the Documents of Vatican II,* vol. 1, ed by Herbert Vorgrimler (New York: Herder and Herder, 1968), p. 13.
18. Pope Paul VI, *Mysterium Fidei*, 40.
19. Pope Paul VI, *Mysterium Fidei*, 44.
20. Issued in the form of a *motu proprio, Solemni hac liturgia* (30 June 1968).
21. Pope Paul VI, *Credo of the People of God*, 25. It has been noted by biographers of Pope Paul VI, especially Peter Hebblethwaite (*Pope Paul VI: The First Modern Pope*), that his thinking was influenced at that time by his friend the French philosopher, Jacques Maritain.
22. See 'The Liturgy of Saint John Chrysostom' in R. C. Jasper and G. J. Cuming, *Prayers of the Eucharist Early and Reformed* (Collegeville: Liturgical Press, 1980, third ed.), p. 133.
23. Cited in Bryan D. Spinks, *Prayers from the East* (Washington: Pastoral Press, 1993), p. 60.
24. Augustine, 'Sermo 272', in Migne, *Patrologia Latina* 38, 1245.
25. Eucharistic Prayer 1 includes a petition: 'Command that these gifts be borne by the hands of your holy Angel to your altar on high in the sight of your divine majesty, so that all of us, who through this participation *at the altar* receive the most holy Body and Blood of your Son, may be filled with every grace and heavenly blessing.' The Latin text says *at this altar,* referring logically to the altar on high and indicating that there is an ambiguity in the English text. While still on earth, the faithful commune with the *risen* Christ at the heavenly table.
26. James Joyce, *Portrait of the Artist as a Young Man* (Ware, Herts: Wordsworth Editions, 1992), pp. 184–5.

5: How Can the People Celebrate Today?

Many who have remained loyal to regular mass attendance are aware of, and inevitably concerned by, the difference between their religious culture and that of a newer generation. They are generally people who, without being able to articulate it, did already have an instinctive Paschal Mystery understanding of the liturgy, though with more awareness of the need to identify with the suffering Christ, as traditional spirituality emphasised. Such a focus on the crucified could hardly result in full appreciation of communion with the risen Lord when receiving the Eucharist. Reliance on the doctrine of transubstantiation has long been a way to cope with questions that instinctively arise and are too difficult to address. This situation differs from what obtained in the early centuries, when Christianity was gradually transforming culture.

The works of the early Church thinkers regularly drew attention to the effects of baptism on those who as adults received the sacrament of enlightenment, as it was called. Hilary of Poitiers (c. 310–c. 367), who became a Christian as a married man, said:

> We who are reborn through the sacrament of baptism have the greatest joy, as we perceive within us the first stirrings of the Holy Spirit, as we understand mysteries.[1]

The 'greatest joy', the 'stirring of the Spirit' and 'understanding (*intelligentia*) of the mysteries' are strong terms, but not unusual descriptions of the adult converts' experience in the early centuries and probably of people in similar circumstances today.

Understanding the mysteries is a big claim, but Hilary's personal testimony does raise the issue of how appropriate is today's pastoral policy of *infant baptism*, as distinct from the policy of *believer's baptism*, common among the Churches of the Evangelical tradition. The sixteenth-century Protestant Reformers who retained infant baptism introduced detailed programmes of catechetical formation to enable children to grow into maturity of the Protestant faith. The Catholic Church already had catechisms of a sort, and after the Council of Trent greatly emphasised this approach, and still does, employing ever changing catechetical programmes, but today many question the adequacy of a policy which seems to be producing many who are 'spiritual' without being religious.

For those who are 'practising' Catholics, it is not enough to attend reverently while a priest says mass. There is effort as well as good will required by those not sufficiently mature in the faith to reach a deep level of participation. And there is a certain cultural burden that stands in the way, as well as less than helpful catechesis and often poorly performed ritual, all of this making participation difficult.[2] The study of helpful teaching resources is important as a remote preparation, and the expression of the intention to participate is fundamental, even if not clearly articulated. It can simply be a desire to encounter Christ, in the whole of the celebration. Traditional prayers of preparation are still valuable, though they tend to be rather individualistic more than an expression of awareness that one is part of the Mystical Body, the subject of the act of worship. Today's young adult generation, highly educated in diverse secular disciplines but catechetically deprived, know instinctively that it is not enough simply to turn up for mass and so do not bother to do so.[3]

Environmental considerations
In the celebration of Word and sacraments, the church's liturgy is performative in the sense that the words and rites bring about an effect in the lives of those who believe, but their effectiveness depends not only on the attitudes and actions of the participants but also on what can be called the environment in which the celebration takes place. As liturgists point out, the nature of the liturgy should determine the form of the architectural space in which it is performed. But that has rarely been true in history. When the Emperor Constantine gave Christianity recognition and preferment, the Church took over public buildings and adapted them to some extent to the needs of liturgical life, and civic architecture has continued to influence church architecture through the ages.[4] Consequently, the physical environment can be helpful or challenging. The Churches of the Eastern Catholic Rite and the Orthodox Church set an example in this regard, with architecture and icons, especially the iconostasis, responding to a human felt need to manifest the sacred visually.

In a notable modern contrast, the Catholic Church in the Netherlands after Vatican II experimented with church architecture designed to lessen the contrast between ecclesiastical and domestic forms, so that the purpose of the church building, both from the outside and the inside, became less obvious than would be true of traditional church architecture.[5]

This approach could find support in 1 Peter 2:4–5:

> Come to (Christ) ... and like living stones let yourselves be built into a spiritual house, to be a holy priesthood, to offer spiritual sacrifices acceptable to God through Jesus Christ.

This implies that when the community celebrates the Eucharist, it is in itself a 'holy' or 'spiritual' house. The beauty which the Psalmist says is found in the Temple, 'I have loved, O Lord, the beauty of your house' (Ps 26:8), is found in the assembly. The assembly must, however, manifest the qualities of truth and love – the other transcendental qualities accompanying beauty – in its liturgical performance.[6] From that perspective, the celebration of the Eucharist can be independent of the physical environment.

Whether specially designed for the liturgy or not, the architectural space needs to be provided with heating, lighting, efficient amplification, some degree of comfortable seating, and these are only the beginning of the requirements. The goodwill and faith of those who come to church require on the part of the presider and collaborators a commitment to provide for their needs. Pope Francis issued a warning:

> Let us be clear here: every aspect of the celebration must be carefully tended to (space, time, gestures, words, objects, vestments, song, music…) and every rubric must be observed. Such attention would be enough to prevent robbing from the assembly what is owed to it; namely, the paschal mystery celebrated according to the ritual that the Church sets down.[7]

Resources need to be expended on the provision of liturgical music (which is not the same as religious music), of vestments and altar furnishing, training of those in active roles, remote preparation in the form of scripture and liturgy groups. The decline in the numbers of clergy may well prove a stimulus to the 'non-ordained' faithful to see to these necessary conditions and so enhance their understanding and their participation.

Secular culture

Other factors enter into consideration of the extent to which the eucharistic rite of today can be effective as a symbolic presentation of the whole Christian mystery. There is the issue of the wider environment of today's secularised culture and the consumerism that makes shopping a seven-day activity. Christians are affected by the levelling down of the traditional difference between Sunday and weekday.

There is a continuous drift towards conforming to secular patterns, as one English commentator noted:

> Holy days of obligation are celebrated on the nearest Sunday so as to avoid inconvenience or the interruption of secular patterns of living. Sunday Mass can be heard on a Saturday to make way for a day's work or cleaning the car or a morning in bed with the papers, like our pagan neighbours.[8]

Sunday is no longer perceived as a festive day, with the result that every day becomes potentially a day for a feast, with special emphasis usually on Friday and Saturday nights. A commentator on the Christian life in the Netherlands observed:

> Through various measures, such as reduction of working hours and early retirement, everyone's share in the work process is reduced, and free time has increased considerably. Leisure is no longer primarily intended to recoup one's strength for work, but has become an end in itself, defining our lifestyle to an ever greater degree.[9]

It is true also that for many the treadmill of the economic machine, to which the individual is enslaved (with 'parole' for the 'weekend') is a dehumanising force extremely difficult to resist, even when people consciously seek a 'work–life' balance. Without a religious culture to give meaning to life, the meaningless nature of a weekend celebration can quickly become evident, and efforts made to enhance it by excess; binge drinking is a symptom of this desperate attempt. From the standpoint of people caught up in such a downward spiral, the Sunday feast can seem not liberating but an expression of reproof, of obligation and control. Various commentators have pointed to perception of the Church's liturgy by many as an expression of a hierarchical world, denoting exclusion of the 'non-ordained', despite the clear thrust of *Sacrosanctum Concilium* towards inclusion and participation.

Morning or evening mass?

A gathering of the community in the morning was part of the earliest Christian tradition, as we learn from the Roman official Pliny the Younger, who reported to the Emperor Trajan from Bithynia (modern Turkey) in 114 that the strange sect called the Christians were

> accustomed to meet before daybreak and to recite a hymn among themselves to Christ, as though he were a god.[10]

He also reported that when their ceremonies were concluded, they were accustomed to 'meet again to take food, but it was of no special character and quite harmless'.[11] From this we could conclude that they probably met again in the evening for a celebration not consisting of a celebratory Jewish type meal followed by a eucharistic celebration but only a simple 'breaking of the bread'.

As the centuries after Pliny's time went on, the practice of meeting morning and evening for prayer, now called the Liturgy of the Hours, became the dominant form of church life in the Roman world, with the celebration of the Eucharist on Sunday a liturgical climax, often prepared for by fasting on Saturday. There is evidence, however, for daily mass in Milan, in the fourth and later centuries,[12] but it seems to have been a privilege of the rich (a priest or bishop was needed) and hardly a widespread occurrence. Receiving communion at home, using portions of the Eucharist brought from the Sunday assembly, was a practice of Basil of Caesarea in the fourth century:

> I communicate four times a week, on the Lord's Day, on Wednesday, on Friday and on the Sabbath, and on the other days if there is a commemoration of any saint.[13]

According to Robert Taft SJ, the practice of communion at home 'lasted among the laity until the seventh century, and even longer in monastic circles'.[14]

The papal mass described in chapter three involved so much ritual that it could only be celebrated on Sunday (or major feast) and for several centuries was the only eucharistic celebration in the city. In other areas, the liturgy of the Word was celebrated, and the unity of the whole community achieved by sending what was called the *fermentum,* bread dipped in the chalice, to the presiders of the other assemblies. Evidence for frequent if not daily mass comes from Augustine in North Africa, and it was probably an evening event. Augustine held that this was of great importance for Christians in times of controversy with dissident groups.[15] Centuries later, daily celebrations took place in the castles of the ninth-century Carolingian Empire, but these were attended only by the resident households and, unlike the case of the Byzantine world, the celebration took place in the morning.[16]

There is little guidance, therefore, available from the early centuries in relation to daily or Sunday celebration, and for what in today's world might be the appropriate time for celebrating the Eucharist. Up to Vatican II, only morning celebrations were allowed, and as the theology of the celebration centred on the historical event of Calvary, that seemed the appropriate time. With the current perception of the festive or meal aspect of the Eucharist, celebration in the evening has an obvious attractiveness, even though a well-celebrated morning mass can highlight the reality of a community meeting to share their lives with Christ and each other in a simple ritual using bread and wine.

The festive nature of the rite becomes clear more easily in the evening, and makes its origin in the Last Supper more evident. I have personal experience of an after-supper Sunday evening mass that created for parishioners a fitting conclusion to the weekend, when emphasis was put on creating a peaceful, gently paced celebration, emphasising the anticipation of the kingdom as the climax of the celebration, when return to the working world of 'Monday' was imminent and would be ethically challenging. It could evoke, too, the situation described in Paul's First Letter to the Corinthians, where festive meals of the Jewish (or Roman) tradition were followed by a simple eucharistic rite.

End-time considerations

Maintaining the idea of the Christian Sunday is quite a challenge, but the Church needs its own 'space' and 'time' in relation to other cultural groups in society and the state. The shared Eucharist should transform the partakers into a distinct body in society, while it is also a local embodiment of the Body of Christ. It is important to remember the relationship between local and universal.

> Each particular church is not an administrative division of a larger whole, but is in itself a 'concentration' of the whole. The whole Catholic Church is qualitatively present in the local assembly, because the whole Body of Christ is present there.[17]

The teaching on the nature of the Church is that it is Catholic, or universal, meaning that it is everywhere in the world, and beyond this world as the heavenly community of saints and the souls undergoing purgation. All are participants in the celebration of the Eucharist, and as a result, the end time, the *eschaton*, the reign of God, is present, though not visibly so in historical time. As John Chrysostom observed (using language typical of Eastern theology):

> For when our Lord Jesus Christ lies slain [as a sacrifice], when the Spirit is with us, when he who sits on the right hand of the Father is here, when sons are made by the washing, when they are fellow-citizens of those in heaven, when we have a country and a city and citizenship there, when we are strangers to things here, how can all these be other than 'heavenly things'?[18]

Paul in the letter to the Colossians saw the Christian life as having at all times this eschatological character:

> If then you have been raised with Christ, seek the things that are above, where Christ is, seated at the right hand of

God. Set your minds on things that are above, not on things that are on earth. For you have died, and your life is hid with Christ in God. (Col 3:1–3)

The Constitution on the Church in the Modern World of the Vatican Council made that point with its statement:

That the earthly and the heavenly city penetrate one another is a fact only open to the eyes of faith.[19]

The text of the Eucharist, especially the Eucharistic Prayer, gives a clear anticipation of the heavenly realm – the 'Holy, Holy, Holy' acclamation is the theme of the perpetual worship of God in heaven. The anticipation in time of the banquet of the kingdom urges the participants to work for inclusiveness among the peoples of the world, transcending cultural and national perspectives. There is need for the Church as community to become more aware of its identity as a harbinger of the end-time, as a body not simply tied down to a role of witnessing to kingdom values in its teaching, but also in its role of helping to realise those values in society.

Being told at the conclusion of the rite: 'Go and announce the gospel of the Lord' is a challenge to engage with the unfinished task of being a leaven in society and an agent of transformation of the world towards its destiny as God's kingdom. In the preface for the Feast of Christ the King, this kingdom is described as 'an eternal and universal kingdom, a kingdom of truth and life, a kingdom of holiness and grace, a kingdom of justice, love and peace'. Properly celebrated, the Sunday feast gives back true meaning to everyday life and the challenges and possibilities it brings.

Digital issues

If you were to ask religiously minded people today whether they thought making religious services available online was a good idea, it is likely that most, nearly all, would agree without a moment's hesitation. There is, however, the issue of whether such access is in itself legitimate. *Sacrosanctum Concilium* referred to 'transmissions of the sacred rites by radio and television, especially television. ... (It) should be done with delicacy and dignity'.[20] Televising religious services, including mass, had taken place before the Council and now has a reasonably long history, making it timely to discuss issues raised by the practice. Televising a concelebration involving quite a number of priests may not be happily regarded by all of them – some may consider close focus on them intrusive. If awkward situations arise unexpectedly, and the camera continues to function, it will be intrusive.

Karl Rahner SJ and the televising of mass

Sacrosanctum Concilium was published in December 1963 and account, therefore, needs to be taken of an article by a leading theologian of the time, Karl Rahner SJ, published in German in 1961 and in an English translation in 1963, in which he argued against televising mass.[21] He asked the question, 'Does the television camera have in principle, from the outset, the same rights as a believing Christian? ... Let us straight away answer that the question, thus put, must be answered with an emphatic No!'[22] His way of stating the question was a little odd; he might have said instead, 'Does the maker of a television programme have in principle ... ?' The human aspect of the event needs to be monitored. He formulated two main arguments. The first hinged on the idea of privacy, though he did not use the word. 'There are things that can be shown at all only if permanently subject to the control, in free consent or refusal, of the person showing them.'[23] The one seeing must participate in a way that involves personal co-operation and not mere curiosity. In that case, there are things that must not be televised, because the person or thing being shown no longer has the possibility of excluding this or that person from this 'self-display'.

> The more personal something is (i.e. the freer it is and the more it involves a man at the deepest level of his being), the more it will lie within the zone of personal intimacy, and thus

be the object of a spiritual sense of modesty, prohibiting the showing of it except as a free utterance, never passing out of the control of the person himself, to the particular person to whom he is addressing himself and who for his part makes an appropriate response to it.[24]

His reference to the 'the particular person' addressed implies person-to-person encounter, but needs to be considered here in the context of televised programmes. Television camera operators today may readily agree with him in relation to what should not be televised, as they are confronted regularly with scenes where the delicacy *Sacrosanctum Concilium* mentions is required – in a situation of profound grief, for example. In practice, television channels observe a code in this regard, now boosted with legislation, though errors of judgement can occur, and the code itself may not be sufficiently rigorous. For example, focusing close up on individuals receiving the Eucharist violates the communicant's privacy, but examples do occur, sometimes specifically because of an individual's identity.

Mass on television

Turning specifically to the mass, Rahner pointed out that it is the most intimate and religious act of which anyone is capable and hedged about with what he called 'a metaphysical sense of modesty'. It therefore requires a quite definite personal participation in faith and love. 'It would be shameless in the highest degree to perform (such a sacred rite) in the sight of any and everyone's indifferent curiosity.'[25] He drew attention to the early Church's *disciplina arcani* (the discipline of the secret), the practice whereby only the baptised could have access to, in the sense of witnessing, the Church's rites, not only the Eucharist but baptism as well.[26] He appealed also to the comment of St Ambrose, the bishop of Milan from 374 to 397, who told how his brother Satyrus did not dare, as an unbaptised person, to witness the Eucharist. He also noted that Thomas Aquinas held that the non-baptised were not allowed even to see the Sacrament of Baptism.[27] I must note at this point that there is an important difference between being physically part of a group celebrating a baptism, while not belonging, not sharing their faith, and witnessing the action by means of the digital media. The old principle, *disciplina arcani*, may be judged to apply in the case of the physical presence of an unbeliever, but it is not obvious that it applies in the other case.

Sound broadcast

In a supplement to his case regarding television, Rahner asked whether 'the microphone does in fact have the same rights as the powers of hearing of the faithful', again a rather convoluted way of asking whether those listening to a sound broadcast can participate as members of the people.[28] His answer was a qualified yes, because he acknowledged that

> a religious sound-broadcast is fundamentally no more than a further technical means of imparting objectified ideas, as is done in a book. In face of the existence of Holy Scripture it is not possible to doubt that the existence of a book with a religious content, indeed the word of God itself, is humanly and morally justified.[29]

There is an obvious difference between broadcasting mass on television and doing so on radio, and yet another between mass on radio and a religious service such as Vespers, this last being an ideal way, when there is appropriate motivation, to participate without being in a position to be physically present. Broadcasting mass on radio can allow all members of the Body of Christ disposed to participate to do so effectively. There is little effective difference between listening to a broadcast of the mass and listening to it in progress in an adjoining room. Clearly those who tune in need to know the structure of the celebration, listen attentively and make an act of spiritual communion. As in the case of the televised mass, there are rules governing the self-display of the one broadcasting. Emotional outbursts on the part of the celebrant would be as unacceptable as they would be on television, while the listener would need to be properly motivated rather than simply curious or carelessly inattentive. If these requirements are satisfied, listeners as members of the Body of Christ can consider themselves part of the people who are celebrating. In fact, listening to a broadcast enables the listener to bypass mental images and generate or create an experience of participation in a way similar to reading a text such as scripture, as Rahner pointed out.

In both physical and online forms, worship needs to have an attractiveness at a level responding to human need, and have more depth than, for example, *Songs of Praise,* to meet those needs. It is clear that a passive watching of worship of some kind on television does not meet that requirement. But how much greater motivation is required? There is plenty of evidence that many people of faith believe they are sharing in the act of worship, to a degree corresponding to their need and requirement as Christians, when they participate online. Especially since the Covid-19 pandemic, being physically present does not have the claim on conscience that existed in the days when people recognised the serious moral obligation to 'attend' Sunday mass. Today most people, perhaps without realising it, are living in the digital age, through the use of the internet to participate virtually in activities taking place elsewhere, and for them the distinction between the 'virtual' and the 'real' is reducing all the time. As Teresa Berger says in *@Worship*:

> A key problem with the assumption that the digital worlds are un-real and illusionary is the underlying distinction between 'virtual' and 'real'. The terms suggest that the digital worlds are un-real while the offline worlds are real. The distinction, however, is both inadequate and outdated.[30]

While maintaining academic objectivity, she does admit to the charm and inviting character of some online religious activities. She cites the example of a labyrinth on the floor of St Paul's Cathedral, London, which visitors to the actual cathedral are invited to enter as a form of pilgrimage with a spiritual and didactic aim.

> The Online Labyrinth, which grew out of an interactive labyrinth on the brick-and-mortar floor ... instructs its digital visitors: 'Please remove your shoes and click here to begin the Labyrinth.'[31]

This is a case where the difference between offline and online, real and virtual, is of little consequence spiritually. The well-known example of the members of prayer groups being linked together online in a way that synchronises the group's worship (perhaps via Zoom) reinforces the case for considering a purely online (or hybrid) act of worship appropriate for today's digital world. The quite real business world has operated in this way for many years, with increasingly advanced technologies employed. As Berger points out, when it comes to worship, exponents of this approach often assert the reality of the online participants' experience because of their bodily involvement in an act of worship. Anecdotal evidence for how spiritually up-building online participation in real time is, comes from the many who through age or infirmity cannot participate physically in church services.

It is a fact that the practice of online worship was well entrenched in the religious culture before the advent of the Covid-19 pandemic. Recent decades have brought a change from the internet world as a source of information to an interactive web-as-platform world. On this platform, new digital worship communities continue to spring up, sometimes in combination with an offline community located in a church building and so enabling shared prayer services. They can be organised in such a way as to make the distinction between offline and online hard to sustain.

Digital ecclesiology
There are many online sites with instructions for the user on how to engage in some ritual, such as making the Sign of the Cross, whether or not this is in conjunction with a service taking place physically and involving a similar ritual. There are sites with no offline

version that use avatars to engage in rituals the online participants are invited to replicate in a service of prayer. There are many other linked offline and online combinations containing prayer services. Because of these possibilities, literature has emerged promoting the idea of the Church as a digital entity, giving rise to the discipline 'digital ecclesiology'.[32] I think it important not to let such thinking lead to understanding the Church simply in digital terms, as if 'digital church' were an adequate description of the catholicity or universality of the Church described above. The digital universe is terrestrial; it does not reach the heavenly world.

The pastoral response to the Covid-19 pandemic included various improvisations and innovations, as pastors endeavoured to provide services online, sometimes combined with outdoor distribution of communion. Pope Francis spoke of this situation during his morning mass celebrated with a small group of the faithful in the chapel of his residence in the Domus Sanctae Marthae on 17 April 2020. He candidly spoke of having received a complaint from a bishop about an arrangement he had sanctioned, mass celebrated in an empty St Peter's Basilica. He now recognised the danger of such arrangements, because people could start living their relationship with God 'for just myself, detached from the people of God'.[33]

He spoke of masses, prayers and faith-based initiatives offered online, with the faithful encouraged to make an act of spiritual communion, given their lack of access to communion, but 'this is not the Church … the Church, the sacraments and the people of God are concrete … May the Lord teach us this intimacy with him, this familiarity with him, but in the Church, with the sacraments, with the holy faithful people of God'.

The Eucharist as a meal

The factual situation of people participating in a way that they find satisfies their spiritual need does mean that Rahner's argument against televising the mass is not totally convincing, especially as *Sacrosanctum Concilium* effectively gave approval to digital participation. The issue should not be decided, however, solely in the context of the present day and the all-pervading digital culture. Unfortunately, the history of the celebration through the ages shows that even with the Council's reform policy some aspects of the nature of the celebration are not sufficiently highlighted. The earliest practice of the 'breaking of the bread' is not fully represented and today's corresponding rite takes place on the altar hardly visible to participants not actually gathered around the altar-table. In any but the smallest gathering, the faithful receive communion in the form of particles produced by a machine.

There is a sense in which, for the celebration of the Eucharist, physical presence is fundamental, given that eating and drinking were the climax of participation from the beginning and belong to the intrinsic nature of the celebration today, and not simply as an individual action to receive nourishment from communion with Christ. That this should be a communal exercise and not simply an individual experience is obvious from the fact that the unity of the community in Christ should result from the gathering, the unity attained through each member being united with Christ and one another in eucharistic communion. A shared meal using bread and wine is transformed to a new order of existence, though for the earth-bound communicants an existence not released from the restraints of time. The rubrics of the present Order of Mass have not highlighted the importance of presenting the celebration as a shared meal centred on real bread and wine, so it is not surprising that the faithful generally do not perceive it in this way.

Eucharistic fast?

It may be that the shortcomings of digital participation will become evident if, at a time of change, people begin to pay more attention to physical aspects of participation. The issue of the eucharistic fast, for example, may arise. For those who actually participate in Church, the fast nowadays before the feast has been very nominal or even non-existent; it is hard to imagine that those who rely on digital participation will have any greater sense of its importance, when they are not physically participating. Yet it formed part of the early Church's ritual, and, in future attempts to provide more authentic celebrations, the importance of it may come to be recognised.

Fasting through the ages was mainly connected with the liturgical cycle of feasts, and it needs to be emphasised that for Christians, whose lives are nourished by the liturgy, this remains the principal role for fasting. Fasting as part of an ascetic lifestyle makes sense in the context of an authentic human life, but from a Christian perspective, fasting can be understood as purification in preparation for a feast, an external manifestation of a more fundamental inner attitude, rather than simply part of an ascetical lifestyle, valuable as that is from a Christian perspective. Thus purified, the Christian can enter joyfully into the feast, in both liturgical and culinary mode.

Conclusion

This chapter has been mainly concerned with the practical issues involved when the eternal Paschal Mystery is celebrated in the varied settings in which the Catholic Church today is acculturated, from villages to megacities, with many others in between. It is surely to be regarded with wonder that what is now called Deep Incarnation – the extent to which the Son God assumed not just humanity but creation in all materiality – has made this possible.[36]

The difficulties encountered in bringing about an authentic celebration may begin, I have suggested, with inadequate catechesis, and may range from physical environment to the restrictions which a secular culture impose on living a truly human Christian life. (Those who are faced with the persecution an ill-disposed secular regime imposes are often energised to create a more-grace filled celebration than free agents may achieve in a liberal democracy.)

In the world of advanced technology, the digital-platforms era has brought its problems as well as its possibilities, leaving some unaware of the importance of physical presence. There is the difficulty that a ritual involving sharing spiritual food derived from the material elements of bread and wine has long been seen in individual terms, with a loss to the realisation of the local Church's unity. In the end the challenge for most people is to learn what the Church teaches about the liturgy and to apply it to the way the Eucharist is celebrated.

Endnotes

1. Hilary of Poitiers, *Tractatus super Psalmos* (Vienna: F. Tempsky, 1891), p. 246 (my translation).
2. See Paul de Clerck, *Vivre et Comprendre la Messe* (Paris: Cerf, 2016).
3. It is salutary to note that, in 1927, Don G. B. Montini, then chaplain to the Italian Federation of Catholic University Students, provided a course on the Church as mystery for them. As Pope Paul VI, it was the subject of his first encyclical, *Ecclesiam Suam* (1964). See Peter Hebblethwaite, *Pope Paul VI: The First Modern Pope*, p. 95.
4. See Thomas O'Loughlin, 'Domestic Ritual, Public Space', in *Shaping the Assembly: How Our Buildings Form Us in Worship*, ed by Thomas O'Loughlin (Dublin: Messenger Publications, 2023), p. 21.
5. Gerard Lukken and Mark Searle, writing about the Church of Ss Peter and Paul, Tilburg, in *Semiotics and Church Architecture* (Kampen: Kok Pharos, 1993), p. 94, stated: 'The visitor has to undertake a process of veridiction, searching for clues as to what sort of a place it is and only finally, by the sort of process of elimination we have conducted here, coming to recognise that it must be a church.'
6. See Thomas O'Loughlin, 'The Welcoming Table, the Beauty of the Temple, and the Disciples of Jesus' in *Worship*, 98 (January 2024), 76–84.
7. Pope Francis, *Desiderio Desideravi*, 23.
8. Eamon Duffy, 'To Fast Again', *First Things*, March 2005.
9. Louis Van Tongeren, 'The Squeeze on Sunday: Reflections on the Changing Experience and Form of Sundays', in P. Post et al., *Christian Feast and Festival: The Dynamics of Western Liturgy and Culture* (Leuven: Peeters, 2001), p. 706.
10. Pliny the Younger, *Letters*, Attalus (website), 10. 96. 9, http://www.attalus.org/old/pliny10b.html.
11. Pliny the Younger, *Letters*, 10. 96. 9.
12. Robert Taft, *Beyond East and West: Problems in Liturgical Understanding* (Washington: The Pastoral Press, 1984), p. 63.
13. Basil of Caesarea, 'Letter 93', in *Nicene and Post-Nicene Fathers*, Second Series, vol. 8, ed by Philip Schaff and Henry Wace (Buffalo, NY: Christian Literature Publishing Co., 1895).
14. Taft, *Beyond East and West*, p. 62.
15. Jungmann, *Mass of the Roman Rite*, p. 179.
16. Jungmann, *Mass of the Roman Rite*, p. 179.
17. William Cavanagh, *Theopolitical Imagination* (London, New York: T & T Clark, 2002), p. 115.
18. John Chrysostom, 'Homily 14 on Hebrews 3', *Nicene and Post-Nicene Fathers*, 1, 14 (Oxford: Parker and Co., 1886), p. 434.
19. *Lumen Gentium*, 40.

20. *Sacrosanctum Concilium*, 20.
21. Karl Rahner SJ, 'The Mass and Television', in *The Christian Commitment: Essays in Pastoral Theology*, trans. by Cecily Hastings (New York: Sheed and Ward, 1963), 205–18. It was first published in German in *Gnade und Sendung* (Innsbruck: Tyrolia Verlag, 1961).
22. Rahner, 'Mass and Television', p. 206.
23. Rahner, 'Mass and Television', p. 206.
24. Rahner, 'Mass and Television', p. 209.
25. Rahner, 'Mass and Television', p. 210.
26. This practice also included a gradual process of instruction of the newly baptised, a deeper formation in the Church's rites, called mystagogy.
27. 'The non-baptised are not even to be allowed to see this sacrament', *The Summa Theologica of St Thomas Aquinas*, part III (London: Burns, Oates and Washbourne, 1914), I q90 a4 ad4, p. 377. Aquinas referred to a statement of Denis the Areopagite, *The Divine Hierarchy*, 7.iii.1: 'Now, if the profane should see or hear that these rites were celebrated by us, they will, I suppose, split with laughter, and compassionate us for our folly. But we need not wonder at this. For, as the Scripture says, "If they will not believe, neither shall they understand."'
28. Rahner, 'Mass and Television', p. 214.
29. Rahner, 'Mass and Television', p. 214.
30. Teresa Berger, *@Worship* (London and New York: Routledge, 2018), p. 16.
31. Cited in Teresa Berger, *@Worship*, p. 17.
32. See for example, *Digital Ecclesiology: A Global Conversation*, ed by Heidi A. Campbell (College Station, Texas: Digital Religion Publications, 2020).
33. 'Pope warns of danger in online masses', *Catholic News Service*, 20 April 2020, www.catholicweekly.com.au/pope-warns-of-danger-in-online-masses.
34. See Dermot A. Lane, *Nature Praising God: Towards a Theology of the Natural World* (Dublin: Messenger Publications, 2022) pp. 79–86.

Epilogue

> The fundamental question is this: how do we recover the capacity to live completely the liturgical action? This was the objective of the Council's reform. The challenge is extremely demanding because modern people – not in all cultures to the same degree – have lost the capacity to engage with symbolic action, which is an essential trait of the liturgical act.[1]

My aim in writing this book has been to empower people to participate in the celebration of the Eucharist with profound awareness that the Paschal Mystery is present in its saving power. It is certainly a lofty aim, but when we read Paul's letters about the nature of the Christian life, a life shared with the risen Christ, it makes us realise that we are adopting a different understanding of human life and religion compared with the common claim to be 'spiritual' but not 'religious'. When the eternal Paschal Mystery appears in time, we must not be surprised if what is happening goes beyond the neat categories to which the non-religious consign ritual activity, insensitive to the power of symbol and regarding participation in church as irrelevant and boring. Those who celebrate in faith must, for their part, take account of the fact that participation is through the power of the Spirit, not just at the high points but all through the celebration, including on occasion long readings or homilies. As a theologian of past centuries taught, it is the Spirit who seals the word of God on our hearts.

In the course of this book, I have drawn attention to the Eastern liturgical tradition with its profound understanding of the symbolic role of the elements of bread and wine, as an alternative to reliance on metaphysical theories concerning substance and accidents. When we recognise the convincing character of the Eastern tradition, the heavenly atmosphere the celebration creates, we may realise that it was the impoverished state of Western scholastic theology over the preceding centuries and not simply reaction to the reductionism of the Reformation or the cautious conservatism of the Roman institution of the time (a story that would have taken too long in the telling) that made the Western liturgical tradition go its separate way and set the Tridentine understanding of the mass in stone. Learning from the East has been part of the renewal of the Western liturgical tradition, while the return to Scripture's centrality and theological renewal, which began a generation before the Vatican Council, has enabled the process of the renewal of the liturgy to occur at and after the Council.

Some of the chapters titles of this book have ended with an interrogation mark; in the case of chapter one this was because the meaning of the word 'people' in the title of the book turned out to be less obvious than might at first appear, more comprehensive than one might expect, and I wanted to stimulate thinking about who might belong to the People of God, the Body of Christ. As an Orthodox theologian has remarked about his own community, 'We know where the Church is, but we cannot be sure about where it is not.'[2]

Many of us who have promoted the ecumenical movement in recent decades have favoured ecumenical convergence through the practice of shared participation in the Liturgy of the Hours – Morning or Evening Prayer, for example. The great tradition of Evensong in the Anglican tradition offers fruitful possibilities in that regard. In a form of ecumenism from the ground up, many practising Catholics now favour a more liberal sharing of liturgical resources, extending even to the Eucharist itself, as they are aware that some members of other Churches are attracted to the Catholic liturgy. This is a sensitive area, and I can do no more than record this feeling on the part of some that the term 'the people' may be more comprehensive than is officially recognised.[3]

Chapter three also asked a question; in this case I was drawing attention to how the understanding of the celebration of the Eucharist went through a radical expansion through considering it a celebration of the Paschal Mystery, a celebration of the saving activity of Christ in his incarnation, passion and resurrection, rather than limiting the perspective to the sacrifice of his life on Calvary. The mass was always a celebration of the Paschal Mystery; it always depended on Christ's resurrection, but the reform of the liturgy of the mass after the Council was needed to make this clear. Communion with the body and blood of the *risen* Christ implies that the fullness of participation comes about not simply by individual reception of Communion but by communal sharing of the Eucharist, thereby manifesting the unity of the Body of Christ, the Church.

Chapter four raised the crucial question of belief in the Eucharist. Controversy surrounded it since about the end of the first millennium and the rise of Protestantism in the sixteenth century caused the Church in the Council of Trent to state its belief by way of reaction. I have asserted that by the early twentieth century the Tridentine teaching had less hold on educated Catholics and that the so-called new theology prepared the way for the great discernment process that marked the Second Vatican Council. The result was a new way to approach the celebration of the Eucharist as a celebration of the Paschal Mystery and consequently a new way of expressing belief in Christ's presence.

In chapter five, I raised the contemporary question of the reality, the extension – and the limits – of participation online. This led to dealing with the potential for participation offered by non-Eucharistic services, and the enhancement of people's spiritual life which may result. But I have been careful not to regard this development as creating a Church in 'cyberspace', as 'digital ecclesiology' would suggest. The digital world is terrestrial; the Church exists both on earth and in heaven, and I do not think that cyberspace can encompass that reality.

Finally, to go back to origins, in chapter two, I mentioned the early emergence of a practice known as the *agape* meal or love feast, which was introduced quite early in the development of the Christian community to foster unity and face the challenges that class division and ethnic differences posed. It is not known how long it lasted, but it was referred to by Clement of Alexandria in the third century.[4] Many centuries later, it was taken up with enthusiasm by the followers of John Wesley (1703–1791), the founder of Methodism in eighteenth-century England. More committed followers, described as 'bands', having no access to Anglican Holy Communion services, developed a way of celebrating their faith and augmenting their sense of mutual love by means of simple rites using bread and non-alcoholic drink or even water. As Methodism gained a foothold as part of the colonisation of America, the use of the love feast spread among those frontier people, beginning with a celebration in 1770 in Philadelphia. The practice was influenced very likely by the fact that Wesley reminded people of the sacral character of daily eating and drinking.[5]

The Methodist Church today experiences the same impact of secular culture on its numbers as other Churches do. While other people's experiences may differ, as culture and personalities do, in my experience something of the warm intimacy of a love feast may be discernible in the environment participants experience in Methodist worship, a factor undoubtedly helpful towards survival in the future. I believe Catholic communities should draw on this situation in some way, when, for example, the assessment of the future prospects of a small rural parish is being made. Rather than relying only on efforts to optimise the performance of the Sunday (or Saturday) celebration of the Eucharist, attention could be focused on a weekday evening gatherings to share stories of personal faith journeys and include such a natural feature as suitable refreshments – this to be done probably in homes rather than sparsely equipped parish facilities.[6] Such a pastoral strategy might well work better in rural rather than urban settings. As a friend has remarked, such gatherings could be nests in which a new Church could grow.

It may prove unwise to speculate about numbers of practising or nominal Catholics and the size of future parish congregations, or about cultural changes in a society that is becoming gradually multicultural, but it is certainly true that liturgical life of the present Catholic community has among its problems a poor level of understanding of its nature. Continuing to provide extensive celebrations of the Eucharist lacking convincing levels of authenticity, as fully participated performances of the Paschal Mystery, seems a dangerous policy and course of action. I believe it is time to reassess schedules and programmes insofar as they exist and have the committed faithful engage instead in a programme of discernment through meetings that manifest the qualities of the early Church's love feast.

Endnotes

1. Pope Francis, *Desiderio Desideravi*, 27.
2. Timothy Ware, *The Orthodox Church* (Harmondsworth: Penguin Books), p. 316.
3. Fintan Lyons, 'Where is the Church', *Doctrine and Life* , January 2001, 8–15.
4. Clement of Alexandria, *Pedagogue*, trans. by Simon Wood (Washington: Catholic University of America Press, 1951), p. 96.
5. Charles Wallace, 'On Knowing Christ in the Flesh', *Wesley and Methodist Studies,* 5 (2013), p. 71.
6. I must admit to having tried this many years ago, without much success; the time was perhaps not right then, but may be now.

Acknowledgements

Thank you to Cecilia West, Brendan McCarthy, Kate Kiernan, Carolanne Henry and all the staff of Messenger Publications for their support in the writing of this book, and thank you to Tom Walsh for his careful reading of the text and very helpful comments.